writing in reality

writing
in reality

James E. Miller, Jr.
University of Chicago

Stephen N. Judy
Michigan State University

Harper & Row, Publishers
NEW YORK, HAGERSTOWN, SAN FRANCISCO, LONDON

Sponsoring Editor: James B. Smith
Project Editor: Eleanor Castellano
Designer: Andrea Goodman
Production Supervisor: Kewal K. Sharma
Compositer: Ruttle, Shaw & Wetherill, Inc.
Printer and Binder: The Murray Printing Company
Art Studio: J & R Technical Services, Inc.

WRITING IN REALITY

Library of Congress Cataloging in Publication Data

Miller, James Edwin, Date-
  Writing in reality.

  Bibliography: p.
  1. English language—Rhetoric. I. Judy, Stephen N.,
joint author. II. Title.
PE1408.M553   808'.042   77-15984
ISBN 0-06-044453-3

acknowledgments

Acknowledgments are made to the following for permission to reprint (the page number given is for the page in this text on which reprinted material appears).

PAGE 6. Andrew Wilkenson, *Spoken English* (Birmingham, England: University of Birmingham, 1965). Copyright © 1965 by the author and the University of Birmingham. Reprinted by permission of the author and *Educational Review*.

PAGE 13. From *Sweet Thursday* by John Steinbeck. Copyright © 1954 by John Steinbeck. Adapted by permission of the Viking Press.

PAGES 13–14. William Carlos Williams, "How I Write," in *New Directions in Prose And Poetry*, ed. James Laughlin. Copyright 1936 by New Directions Publishing Corporation. Reprinted by permission of the publisher.

PAGE 16. Herbert R. Kohl, *Teaching the Unteachable*. Reprinted with permission from the New York Review of Books. Copyright © 1967 Herbert Kohl.

PAGES 16–17. LeRoi Jones, "LeRoi Jones Talking," from *Home: Social Essays*. New York: William Morrow & Company. Reprinted by permission.

PAGES 21–22. Carl Jung. *Man and His Symbols*. © 1964 Aldus Books, London. Reprinted by permission.

PAGES 27–28. From *Times Three* by Phyllis McGinley. Copyright © 1952 by Phyllis McGinley. Originally appeared in *The New Yorker*. Reprinted by permission of the Viking Press.

PAGE 28. "Fifteen" from *The Rescued Year* by William Stafford. Copyright © 1964 by William E. Stafford. By permission of Harper & Row, Publishers.

PAGES 36, 41, 52, 88. "When I Read The Book," "A Noiseless Patient Spider," and excerpt from "Song of Myself" from Walt Whitman, *Complete Poetry and Selected Prose*, ed. James E. Miller, Jr. (Boston: Houghton Mifflin, Company, 1959). Reprinted by permission.

PAGES 38–39. Langston Hughes, *The Big Sea*. Reprinted with permission of Hill and Wang (now a division of Farrar, Straus & Giroux, Inc.) Copyright 1940 by Langston Hughes.

PAGES 41, 108. Poetry of Emily Dickinson reprinted by permission of the Trustees of Amherst College from *The Poems of Emily Dickinson*, edited by Thomas H. Johnson, Cambridge, Mass.: The Belknap Press of Harvard University Press, Copyright © 1951, 1955 by the President and Fellows of Harvard College.

PAGES 52, 59. "Wondering" and "Teacher" from *Miracles*. Copyright © 1966 by Richard Lewis. Reprinted by permission of Simon and Schuster, Inc.

PAGE 54. Ruth Lechlinter, "Drawing by Ronnie, C., Grade One." Copyright © 1967 by Saturday Review, Inc. Reprinted by permission of the publisher.

PAGES 54–55, 66. Charles Reznikoff, *By the Waters of Manhattan*. Copyright, 1937, 1934, by Charles Reznikoff. Reprinted by permission of New Directions Publishing Company.

PAGE 58. James Thurber, "Daugerrotype of a Lady," from *The Thurber Album*. Copyright © 1952, James Thurber. Published by Simon and Schuster. Originally printed in *The New Yorker*. We also acknowledge the gracious assistance of Mrs. Helen Thurber.

PAGE 59. "About the House," by J. M. *The New Yorker*, September 10, 1966. Copyright © 1966 by The New Yorker. Reprinted by permission of the publisher.

PAGE 64. From "The Bald Soprano" by Eugene Ionesco. Reprinted by permission of Grove Press, Inc. Copyright © 1956 by Eugene Ionesco. Copyright © 1958 by Grove Press, Inc.

PAGE 84. "If We Must Die," from *Selected Poems of Claude McKay*: Copyright © 1953 by Twayne Publishers, Inc. and reprinted with the permission of Twayne Publishers, a division of G. K. Hall & Co., Boston.

PAGE 86. William Faulkner, "Acceptance Speech for Nobel Prize," from *Essays, Speeches, and Public Letters*, ed. James B. Meriwether (New York: Random House, Inc., 1965). Reprinted by permission of the publisher, Random House, Inc.

PAGE 88. Paul Reps, ed. *Zen Flesh, Zen Bones: A Collection of Zen and Pre-Zen Writings* (Rutland, Vermont, and Tokyo: Charles E. Tuttle, Inc., 1957). Reprinted by permission of Charles E. Tuttle.

PAGE 97. B.C. by permission of Johnny Hart and Field Enterprises, Inc.

PAGE 122. William Carlos Williams, *Collected Earlier Poems.* Copyright, 1938 by New Directions Publishing Corporation.

PAGES 124–125. "In the Dark," from *Now We Are Six* by A. A. Milne. Copyright, 1927, by E. P. Dutton & Co. Renewal © 1955 by A. A. Milne. Reprinted by permission of the publishers, E. P. Dutton.

PAGES 127–128. "Ravin's of Piute Poet Poe," from *American Literature in Parody,* ed. by Robert P. Falk. Copyright © 1972 by Tawyne Publishers and reprinted by permission of Twayne Publishers, a division of G. K. Hall & Co., Boston.

PAGES 135–136. Geneva Smitherman, "Soul 'N Style" from *English Journal,* March 1974. Copyright © 1974 by the National Council of Teachers of English. Reprinted by permission of the publisher.

PAGE 140. George Orwell, "Politics and the English Language," from *Shooting an Elephant and Other Essays,* published by Harcourt, Brace, Jovanovich, Inc.

PAGES 149–150. Excerpt from *McLuhan: Hot & Cool,* edited by Gerald Emmanuel Stearn. Copyright © 1967 by Gerald E. Stearn. Copyright © 1967 by Marshall McLuhan. Reprinted by permission of the Dial Press.

contents

preface

Writing in Reality has its roots in another book written by James E. Miller, Jr., *Word, Self, Reality: The Rhetoric of the Imagination* (Dodd, Mead, 1972). Although some of the language has been carried over, this book's principal debt is to the philosophy of writing instruction evolved in *Word, Self, Reality:* to use Miller's phrase, "spinning the reader, again and again, out of his own orbit into other orbits—intellectual, imaginative, linguistic—for deeper exploration and personal discovery."

Part I of *Writing in Reality* is titled, "Explorations: The World in Words." It consists of ten chapters designed to engage writers in an exploration of the self and the world through language, beginning with self-awareness and personal writing, extending into public worlds and public writing, yet returning in the end to consider writing and "the ultimate self." Part II, "Extensions: Words in the World," asks the reader to engage in a more formal examination of the raw materials of composition—language and thinking—and to consider the ways in which language is shaped by, and shapes, human thought.

Although we have arranged the chapters in what we feel is a practical order based on our experiences of teaching writing, each chapter is designed to stand alone and to be taught independently. Instructors may well want to create their own order by intermixing chapters, particularly those from Parts I and II. For example, Chapter 13 on "Language Play" might be introduced early in the program with Chapter 1 on "Personal Writing." "Creating Order out of Chaos" (Ch. 12) might be meshed with "Encountering the World" (Ch. 6), and "Language, Society, and Morality" (Ch. 15) makes a natural companion to "Causes and Commitments" (Ch. 9). The discussion of correctness in writing found in "Language and Community" (Ch. 14) may usefully be taken up early in a course.

In each chapter we present three kinds of activities for students: Sections labeled *Discussion* invite the reader to consider the nature of language, of the writing process, and of words in the world and provide a starting point for small- and large-group class discussions; *Writing Ideas and Experiments,* or in Part II, *Ideas and Experiments,* present a variety of writing projects (an interesting and challenging variety, we think); *Further Points of Departure* include supplementary reading, writing, and discussion topics which, at the option of student or instructor, can considerably enlarge the range and depth of a writing course.

Throughout the book we have placed particular emphasis on helping writers contemplate, and develop consciousness of, their writing and their mastery of the writing process. For example, in the Introduction to Part I, we make explicit our own assumptions about the teaching and learning of writing and invite the reader to discuss and debate them. If such activities are pursued regularly throughout the program, the reader will be led to develop what amounts to his or her own "text" on writing, a "rhetoric of the imagination" describing the individual's encounter with words in the world.

A very popular feature of *Word, Self, Reality* was the use of epigraphs and quotations from writers, linguists, philosophers, and others presenting a range of views about language and writing. That collection has been considerably expanded and broadened in *Writing in Reality.* The writers represented include: Martin Luther King, Jr., Lewis Carroll, Samuel Johnson, Arthur Conan Doyle, Anthony Trollope, Claude McKay, Ralph Ellison, Eugene Ionesco, Virginia Woolf, Bashō, William Shakespeare, Gertrude Stein, Joyce Carol Oates, John Gunther, Charles Reznikoff, Thomas Hood, Robert Burns, Walt Whitman, Emily Dickinson, Hermann Hesse, Langston Hughes, Lorraine Hansberry, Ernest Hemingway, Jean Stafford, Willa Cather, William Stafford, Phyllis McGinley, Edgar Allan Poe, LeRoi Jones, Henry David Thoreau, Eldridge Cleaver, William Carlos Williams, Wolcott Gibbs, Henry James, D. H. Lawrence, Pearl Buck, Cardinal Richelieu, Jonathan Swift, Goethe, Pliny, Johnny Hart, William

Faulkner, Mark Twain, and Alexander Pope. Commentators from the fields of linguistics, anthropology, philosophy, psychology, and social science include: Martin Buber, Wendell Johnson, Clifton Fadiman, Andrew Wilkinson, James Britton, S. I. Hayakawa, Edward Sapir, Carl Jung, Abraham Maslow, Ernst Cassirer, William James, L. S. Vygotsky, Alfred North Whitehead, Wilhelm Stekel, Martin Heidegger, R. W. Gerard, Clyde Kluckhohn, R. D. Laing, Alfred Korzybski, George Orwell, Raven McDavid, Weller Embler, Theodore Roszak, Geneva Smitherman, John B. Carroll, Robert Pooley, Marshall McLuhan, John Gardner, Robert Maynard Hutchins, Charles Weingartner, Neil Postman, Claude Levi-Straus, Dennis Gabor, André Breton, and Alan McGlashan.

We wish to thank Susan Koch, Central Michigan University, and Gilbert Tierney, Harper College, for reading and commenting on the manuscript in its early stages; David Mead of Michigan State University for his interest and support throughout the project; Alice Crouch and Janice Masucci for manuscript preparation; and Eleanor Castellano of Harper & Row for her editorial work. Special thanks go to our poetry consultant, Stephen Patrick Judy, for his advice on selections from the works of A. A. Milne.

STEPHEN N. JUDY   JAMES E. MILLER, JR.

I

explorations:
the world
in words

INTRODUCTION: SOME ASSUMPTIONS ABOUT
THE TEACHING AND LEARNING OF WRITING

Why did I write? What sin to me unknown
Dipt me in ink, my parents' or my own?
ALEXANDER POPE, Epistle to Dr. Arbuthnot

Composition is, for the most part, an
effort of slow diligence and steady
perseverence, to which the mind is
dragged by necessity or resolution.
SAMUEL JOHNSON, The Adventurer #138

Write without pay until somebody offers
to pay. If nobody offers within three
years, the candidate may look upon his
circumstance with the most implicit
confidence as the sign that sawing
wood is what he was intended for.
MARK TWAIN, A General Reply

He [the writer] must teach himself that
the basest of all things is to be
afraid, and, teaching himself that,
forget it forever, leaving no room in
his workshop for anything but the old
verities and truths of the heart, the
old universal truths lacking which any
story is ephemeral and doomed—love
and honor and pity and pride and
compassion and sacrifice.
WILLIAM FAULKNER, Nobel Prize Acceptance Speech

Writing is busy idleness.
GOETHE, Gotz von Berlichen

You can't write writing.
WENDELL JOHNSON, "You Can't Write Writing"

Too much polishing weakens rather than
improves a work.   PLINY, Epistles

Blot out, correct, insert,
refine,
Enlarge, diminish, interline;
Be mindful when invention fails
To scratch your head, and bite your
nails.

JONATHAN SWIFT, *On Poetry*

Give me six lines written by the most
honorable of men, and I will find an
excuse in them to hang him.

CARDINAL RICHELIEU

Perhaps no question has caused greater perplexity for both
teachers and students than the deceptively simple: "How do
people learn to write?" Many argue that writing can be
learned only through a painful, disciplined sequence of
carefully prescribed writing assignments with error correc-
tion by the instructor. Others claim that writing can be
learned only if the writing process is made engaging and
pleasurable for the student. Emerson believed: "All writing
comes by the grace of God"; Samuel Johnson asserted that
"scribendo disces scribere"—you learn to write by writing.
Pearl Buck recommended "writing without criticism";[1]
Clifton Fadiman advised teachers to "correct every error,
with reasons; do not coddle. . . ."[1] William Cobbett argued,
"Never think of mending what you write."

Some people cut through the problem by dismissing it:
"Why bother? Nobody can teach writing anyway."

This confusion has had the effect of creating an enormous apprehension of writing courses. All too many people
come to writing courses in colleges and universities with a
sense of fear and dread, persuaded by past experiences that
they are incompetent writers, doomed to failure. Such fears
have not been reduced by the fact that for years writing
teachers in both high school and college have taken a hard-

[1] Lee Frank Lowe, "Writers on Learning to Write," *English Journal,*
October 1964.

line approach, berating students for what they see as the inadequacies and deficiencies in their writing.

Neither casting blame nor making people feel uncomfortable about themselves and their writing solves the problem or leads to sensible answers to the question: "How do people learn to write?"

One way to attack the question is to look at its negative: "How *don't* people learn to write?" We are convinced that writing instruction has too often focused on the form of writing rather than on the writer and the writing process. Therefore, in writing this book we have not included a great deal of discussion of "proper" language, the usual lists of "do's" and "don'ts"—restraints and regulations—about language. Language is essential in our lives and too important in our fate to reduce it to a matter of good grammar or refined propriety. This is not a book, then, about when to use *who* or *whom*, or when you might get by with saying *ain't*, or when to use *like* and when to use *as*.

We agree in some respects with those who say "you can't teach writing," if by that is meant that you can't make a person master of the writing process through lectures and drills or by pointing out errors, flaws, and "blights" in the writing. However, on the basis of our own teaching, we are convinced that the process of writing—idiosyncratic though it may be—can be mastered quite successfully by most people, provided the needs and interests of the writer are placed at the center of instruction.

What this book attempts to do, then, is to provide opportunities for you to engage productively in the act of writing and to help you develop an awareness both of the mystery and potential of language and of your own control of it.

Here are our basic assumptions about the teaching and learning of writing. We invite you to consider them, discuss them, debate them, to test them against your own experience. In other words, before we set you to the task of writing, we believe you should think about the assumptions underlying what we ask you to do.

• • •

The first of our assumptions is that writing must be ① *motivated* (and that the best writing is deeply motivated); therefore, any attempt to induce writing must begin by tapping feelings and experiences. Another way of saying this is presented in Chapter 1, where we suggest that all good writing is *personal,* whether it be an abstract essay or a private love letter. Writing which is unmotivated and impersonal lacks vibrancy and involvement. Unless you tap the inner sources, no amount of theme practice will ever help you write more successfully.

A second assumption is that once your writing is moti- ② vated, you will find language resources that will help you say what you want to say. We feel no need to teach you about language, because you already know an astonishing amount about it from actual use. You have been spinning sentences all your life; it would be redundant and wasteful of us to reteach that. You have the language; our aim is to help you release and control it.

A third assumption is that people develop control over words as they use language for exploration of inner worlds ③ and for making connections with others in dialogue and discussion. In making contact with others, human beings shape their language for particular purposes. We feel that organization, structure, style, and appropriateness evolve as people struggle to communicate with one another.

A fourth assumption is that particularly in the early phases of a writing program, discussions of correctness in ④ language should be kept to a minimum. While the demands placed on writers for surface correctness—good grammar, proper spelling and punctuation—deserve careful consideration, they must be placed in a subsidiary position to writing itself. The issues and problems connected with standard English and its use are indeed complex, and several chapters in Part II of this book are devoted to it. We don't mean to suggest that you ignore the conventions of writing altogether, turning in illegible, unpunctuated, misspelled papers in this or any other course. But we do believe that the desire for correctness will emerge when you strongly want a hearing from those readers who demand such propriety.

• • •

Underlying all these assumptions is our belief that the mystery and magic of language are, in large part, the mystery and magic of the processes of the imagination. Probably there is no use of language that does not involve some part of the imagination; and conversely, the imagination finds some of its finest manifestations in language.

The development of the personality is inextricably bound up with the development of language. Language is the basic and essential instrument in the humanising of the species; without it thought above very primitive levels is impossible. Language and man are in continual interaction; change the man in some way and you change the language he uses; change the language he uses and you change the man. On the one hand the process of growth through education and experience causes him to reach out for new language in which to understand and communicate. On the other hand this language contains new thoughts and shades of thought, new feeling and shades of feeling which help to determine such growth. His ability to direct rather than to be directed by experience, his ability to establish human relationships, are intimately related to his capacity for language; the frustrations of the inarticulate go deep. And it must be borne in mind that "language" in this context is overwhelmingly the spoken language; even in the (historically) rare literate societies such as our own this remains true. Without oracy human fulfillment is impossible; speech and personality are one.

ANDREW WILKINSON, *Spoken English*

For too long the assumption has been made that language used by an individual originates in the orderly processes of a rational mind. Instruction in writing has, therefore, been aimed largely at this logical faculty in the belief that the teaching of orderly processes will result in good writing. The result, as we have implied, has too often been not good writing but dead writing, inhibited and restrained, and frequently dehumanized and unreadable. It is writing *correct* in most respects, but alive in none.

The processes of the imagination, like many of the workings of the human mind, remain shrouded in mystery. Many great creative minds have testified to this mystery and have expressed their awe of it. Henry James, in describing the way an idea for a story came to him, says that all of a sudden he found himself in possession of his material:

> The whole cluster of items forming the image is on these occasions born at once; the parts are not pieced together, they conspire and interdepend; but what it really comes to, no doubt, is that at a simple touch an old latent and dormant impression, a buried germ, implanted by experience and then forgotten, flashes to the surface as a fish, with a single "squirm," rises to the baited hook, and there meets instantly the vivifying ray.
>
> HENRY JAMES, *The Art of the Novel*

Few of us have written novels or even attempted to, but the role of the imagination is similar in all kinds of writing, from essay to poem to novel. The process of the imagination is probably the most important part of the process of writing—and it is a part that has been virtually ignored by handbooks on composition.

A FINAL NOTE: WRITING AND REALITY

Having read this discussion, you may well have a very important question in mind: "Does a writing program that centers on the imagination prepare a person for the realities of the writing world?" Or, phrasing it another way: "Is there any reason to believe that the time spent in imaginative writing experiences will carry over to the 'real world'—especially to college and business—where the writing demanded is, as often as not, quite pedestrian and unimaginative?"

To both questions we emphatically answer, "yes," and this leads us to the final assumption on which this book is based: A person who has a rich variety of writing experiences, is conscious of the mysteries of the imagination, yet is confident in his or her own experience and imagination will be successful in dealing with the writing demands of reality; conversely, a student who has received exclusive training in so-called practical forms may, ironically, be limited in the ability to write those forms successfully, limited by the very narrowness of the experience. It may well be that after you finish college, you will never be called upon (or have the desire) to write anything more elaborate than a memo or report. Nevertheless, if you engage in a variety of imaginative writing experiences and if that engagement is personally satisfying, we think you will have enormously extended both your power over the written word—the pedestrian as well as the creative—and deepened your own sense of self. Nothing, we think, can be more practical than that.

DISCUSSION

Individuals have different feelings about the writing process. Using the following questions as a guide, think through your own feelings: Do you approach a writing task with a sense of fear and repulsion? with vigor and enthusiasm? Why? What kinds of writing give you most satisfaction? which least? Do you ever write poems, plays, or stories on your own? To what extent are your concerns about writing similar to those of other people in the course?

We have outlined our basic assumptions about the teaching and learning of writing. To what extent do they mesh with your own set of beliefs about writing? (Perhaps your instructor will offer his or her own set for you to consider.)

Review the epigraphs that begin this introduction. Though some are obviously facetious, others offer ideas that other writers will find helpful. Which ring true for you?

Explore the implications of Wilkinson's assertion that the "development of the personality is inextricably bound up with the development of language."

Try to recollect some of the advice you have received about your own writing, advice about structure, correctness, organization, creativity, beginnings/middles/endings, topic sentences, outlines, paragraph structure, and so on. Which advice has proven useful to you? Which has actually inhibited your use of language?

Talk over some of the topics you can recall having written about in junior or senior high school. Which "worked" for you? Which didn't? Why? (How many times did you have to write on the topic: "My Summer Vacation"?)

1

Personal writing

> The only man I ever knew who claimed
> that composition gave him no pain
> was a very bad writer, and he is now
> employed in a filling station.
>
> WOLCOTT GIBBS

A PRELIMINARY QUESTION—WHY WRITE?

At the beginning of any book on writing, the question should be posed: "Why write?" There was a time, in prehistory, when people did not write. There are primitive tribes now in existence whose languages—often very sophisticated and complex—remain totally oral. But in our bewildering technological, electronic culture, reading and writing are matters of survival. What one becomes will depend to a surprising degree on the mastery of these processes, not simply what one becomes in the sense of an occupation or profession, but also what one becomes as an individual human being.

No abstract generalization is so persuasive as an individual case; in *Soul on Ice*, Eldridge Cleaver explained that writing was simply a matter of salvation:

That is why I started to write. To save myself. I realized that no one would save me but myself. The prison authorities were both uninterested and unable to help me. I had to seek out the truth and unravel the snarled web of my motivations. I had to find out who I am and what I want to be, what type of man I should be, and what I could do to become the best of which I was capable.

     ELDRIDGE CLEAVER, "On Becoming," *Soul on Ice*

It is doubtful that anyone could formulate a better reason for writing—*to seek out the truth and unravel the snarled web of our motivations*. That is perhaps enough justification. If we find out who we are or what we can become, writing performs an even more crucial role: not to get a grade or pass a course, but to sound the depths, to explore, and to discover.

> [My works] are things I wrote to main-
> tain myself in a world much of which
> I didn't love. I had to fight to
> keep myself as I wanted to be.
> WILLIAM CARLOS WILLIAMS, *Selected Letters*

Critical though writing is to our becoming, too few people have been willing to admit that the writing process is a mystery. Often writing is deeply and richly rewarding, but frequently it is exasperating and exhausting, beset with problems. The most obvious problem is simply the flow of words from the self to the page—the flow that rushes at times, slows at other times to a sluggish pace. There are occasions when we can channel the flow easily with force and direction, when we are supremely conscious and in control of everything the stream of words carries; but on other occasions the flow is stubborn, ignoring any orders from the conscious mind and turning in directions that we had not wanted or anticipated. Although we are sometimes pleased at writing what we set out to write, we can often be surprised at writing something that we did not intend and perhaps do not even fully understand.

Doc bought a package of yellow pads and two dozen pencils. He laid them out on his desk, the pencils sharpened to needle points and lined up like yellow soldiers. At the top of a page he printed: OBSERVA- TIONS AND SPECULATIONS. His pencil point broke. He took up another and drew lace around the O and the B, made a block letter of the S and put fish hooks on each end. His ankle itched. He rolled down his sock and scratched, and that made his ear itch. "Someone's talking about me," he said and looked at the yellow pad. He wondered whether he had fed the cotton rats. It is easy to forget when you're thinking. . . .

Doc remembered that he had not eaten. When he finished a page or two he would fry some eggs. But wouldn't it be better to eat first so that his flow of thought would not be interrupted later? For some days he had looked forward to this time of peace, of unbroken thought. These were the answer to his restlessness: peace and the life of the mind. It would be better to eat first. He fried two eggs and ate them, staring at the yellow pad under the hanging light. The light was too bright. It reflected painfully on the paper. Doc finished his eggs, got out a sheet of tracing paper, and taped it to the bottom of the shade below the globe. It took time to make it neat. He sat in front of the yellow page, and threw it away. Five pencil points were broken now. He sharpened them and lined them up with their brothers. . . .

He set his jaw and was starting to turn back to his desk when he saw out of the corners of his eyes the flash of a skirt. He looked out the window again. A girl . . . was walking along Cannery Row toward Monterrey. Doc couldn't see her face, but she had a fine walk, thigh and knee and ankle swinging free and proud, no jerk and totter the way so many women walked as they fell from step to step. No, this girl walked with her shoulders back and her chin up and her arms swinging in rhythm. It's a gay walk, Doc thought. You can tell so much by a walk—discouragement or sickness, determination. There are squinched-up mean walks and blustering walks, shy creeping walks, but this was a gay walk, as though the walker were going happily to a meeting with someone she loved. There was a pride in the walk, too, but not vanity. Doc hoped she would not turn the corner, but she did. There was a flick of skirt and she was gone. But Doc could see in his mind her swinging limbs, the melody of her lithe, swift movement. Probably ugly as a mud fence, he thought, and then he laughed at himself. "That's full circle," he said. "Mind, I congratulate you. You jumped me to sex, translated it to aesthetics, and ended with sour grapes. How dishonest can I be? And all because I don't want to go to work. I'll work my head off to avoid work. Come mind. This time you don't get away with it—back to the desk."

JOHN STEINBECK, *Sweet Thursday*

The emotions of writing—of attempting to write—are surprisingly varied and deeply felt. Like Steinbeck's Doc, most of us find something intimidating about an empty page ready to be used. Even when we are filled with a subject, idea, or emotion that we want to express, it takes a major act of will and physical self-discipline to begin making the black marks on the white paper. If the flow of words runs smoothly and we like what we say after we say it, we may have that feeling of elation that is peculiar to writing well—a sense of self-fulfillment in creation. And as the feeling gives us satisfaction and confidence, the flow increases, and writing begins to seem almost effortless.

One takes a piece of paper, anything,
the flat of a shingle, slate, cardboard

and with anything handy to the purpose
begins to put down the words after
the desired expression in mind.   This
is the anarchical phase of writing.
The blankness of the writing surface
may cause the mind to shy, it may be
impossible to release the faculties.
Write, write anything: it is in all
probability worthless anyhow, it
is never hard to destroy written
characters.   But it is absolutely
essential to the writing of anything
worthwhile that the mind be fluid and
release itself to the task.
              WILLIAM CARLOS WILLIAMS, "How to Write"

Sometimes it is possible to trick the flow into starting. The trick might be as simple a thing as writing whatever comes into the mind—making free associations—to set the creative energies flowing. Making a list of random thoughts might work, and they can be sorted through later, put in order, discarded, or revised. Tricks can include such oblique approaches as a yoga session or a walk in the park. There is no reason not to try some of these strategies, and you may also find some that no one else has thought of. It is important for you to discover your own style, one which allows you to write when you need to with some degree of comfort and self-assurance. Some people can write only at night, plowing along 'til dawn's early light. Others work best in the morning. A few happy souls can—when the moment comes— sit at a typewriter and bat out polished prose. Most, alas, struggle along, fighting for word after word.

One problem many writers have is simply a lack of confidence in themselves. "Who'd ever want to read what I've got to say?" "I've never thought or done anything significant." They think this way; then instead of writing from within, they force themselves to write about the unfamiliar, which produces a good deal of selfless gobbledygook.

All good writing, we think, is *personal* writing. Someone, puzzled by the term *personal experience*, once remarked: "I've never had an experience that wasn't personal." This view may well be applied to writing. What is personal writing? It is writing which requires a single individual to speak with his or her own voice of his or her own experience. The person may speak on any subject, choose any method or form, and fulfill any chosen purpose. The one constant that runs through all good writing is the writer's voice, the distinctive accent transferred from the depths of the self to the blank sheet of paper.

A good essay, research paper, or memo, written with originality, purpose, and imagination, is highly personal writing even though it may be phrased in formal language; and any of these written without personal engagement is likely to be flat, uninteresting, and dull.

Many people have been indoctrinated to believe that good writing is primarily correct writing and that the best writing is objective and impersonal (and therefore devoid of the first-person singular). As a result, there is abroad an ideal prose so correct, objective, and impersonal that it is almost unreadable. This prose pours out of government offices, universities, and businesses; it is faceless and voiceless—the inhuman sound that arises from it is monotonous and boring. Often an attempt is made to make it seem, not the sound of a human voice, but the proclamation of an establishment or the oracular declaration of an organization. The following passage, for example, has been taken from a government document explaining the operation of a series of clearinghouses established to handle the great flood of scholarship on education:

The nearly explosive expansion of education resources has triggered an equivalent proliferation of written material. A significant proportion of what is currently appropriate and of merit too often is not reported in sources readily available to the greatest number of potential users. There is a need for a comprehensive and structured means of information exchange. Methods must be found for organizing and distilling this information in order more effectively to channel the efforts of researchers and practitioners toward the utilization of all available data and resources. Experience suggests that there would be unnecessary duplication and wasted effort if information handling agencies or clearinghouses were to develop autonomously. The problem, consequently, reduces to one of establishing a network of specialized clearinghouses designed to meet the need for information retrieval in education while avoiding the hazards of independent development. To this end the Educational Research Information Center of the United States Office of Education is developing a network of information centers in the field of education so that information may be most efficiently acquired, stored, retrieved and exchanged among the cooperating units and other members of the educational community.
U.S. Department of Health, Education, and Welfare

Few people will be lured into reading beyond the first line of this passage. It is not only monotonous but also pompous. It achieves a kind of pseudo-objectivity by repressing all personal reference in its pretentious vocabulary and its elaborate statement of the obvious.

What is the sound of the personal voice in writing? It is perhaps easier to show than to describe. Henry David Thoreau's voice sounds loud and clear in his work, and the tone can be caught in a single sentence: "I would rather sit on a pumpkin and have it all to myself than be crowded on a velvet cushion."[1]

The sound of the human voice also comes through in this paragraph by an eleven-year-old Harlem resident:

My block is the most terrible block I've ever seen. There are at least
25 or 30 narcartic people in my block. The cops come around there
and tries to act bad but I bet inside of them they are as scared as can
be. They even had in the papers that this block is the worst block,
not in Manhattan but in New York City. In the summer, they don't
do nothing except shooting, shaving, and fighting. They hang all
over the stoops and when you say excuse me to them they hear you
but they just don't feel like moving. Some times they make me so
mad that I feel like slaping them and stuffing an bag of garbage
down their throats. Theres only one policeman who can handle these
people and we all call him "sunny." When he come around in his cop
car the people run around the corners, and he wont let anyone sit
on the stoops. If you don't believe this story come around some time
and you'll find out.

                    HERBERT R. KOHL, *Teaching the "Unteachable"*

And here is the sound of the human voice in a passage from LeRoi Jones:

For those of you who do not know my name, I am what is called
"A Negro Writer." I write what is commonly called "Negro Literature."
What these terms usually mean (I mean somewhere below the veil of
anxious politeness smart Americans think of as their image) is that
the people who can be tagged with them produce a variety of writing
that should be thought of as second rate, in much the same way all
American literature was thought of before Melville, Poe, James, etc.
But the reasons for this low estimate of black writing have not, I
think, been fully understood. And I mean the estimate made by the

[1] Henry David Thoreau, *Walden and Civil Disobedience*, ed. Owen Thomas (New York, W. W. Norton & Co., 1966), p. 25.

official estimators, the deciders of what is of intellectual, hence emotional, value in the society, *i.e.*, what can be carried off and deposited in that huge junk heap of useless artifacts called Culture.

LE ROI JONES, *Home: Social Essays*

In coming weeks and months (and years) you will be writing a number of short and long papers—some will be private explorations of deep concerns; others, public discussions of issues and events—all, it is to be hoped, with the vigor and directness that grow from confidence in using your own voice.

DISCUSSION

Why write? In an age of telephone, radio, television, and film, why write? Consider Cleaver's description of his writing "for salvation." Can this hold true for you? Without stretching a point, consider reasons for writing other than meeting the demands placed on people by school, college, and industry.

Review your own writing habits and compare them with those of others in your class. When, where, and how do you write most comfortably? Do you write drafts in longhand or on the typewriter? Do you prepare a smooth or rough first draft? Do you pace the floor or sit quietly working? Can you write while listening to music? Must you? Can you concentrate through noise or commotion? Can you write in absolute silence? Do you need deadlines as a source of inspiration? What are the highly individual traits you have developed as a writer?

Describe as vividly as you can some of the actual experiences you have had writing a paper. Discuss writing experiences that have been especially satisfying to you. What was the source of the pleasure? What is the most difficult writing experience you can recall? What made it so?

Discuss how the creative flow begins. How do you get started writing? What are the tricks of the trade you have evolved?

Have you been taught never to use first-person pronouns in essays? How does this affect your personal voice? (As an experiment, try telling someone an important thought or feeling without using the word "I." What limitations does this place on your ability to communicate?)

Bring to class several pieces that you have written in the past. Try to discover your own voice in your writing. Can you define its character? Which of your papers do others believe best reflect your true voice? (By way of contrast, look at your voice as it emerges in your friendly letters. How does it differ?)

WRITING IDEAS AND EXPERIMENTS

When ideas refuse to flow, remember that language may be the best spur to thought. One way to let language flood in and get the mind moving is to sacrifice the first sheet of paper to doodling and experimenting, writing down whatever comes to mind, then writing down what that brings to mind, and then jumping over to a completely unrelated notion and jotting that down. "Get black on white," as de Maupassant advised. The following exercises not only limber up the fingers and reduce white-paper panic, but start the flow, and if luck holds, turns it into a flood that cannot be dammed!

Try flipping through the dictionary and letting a chance-encountered word start off a train of associations—*hairball, helpmate, levee, marksman, nothing, sigh.*

Try "automatic" writing, letting the pen move across the page creating sentences that are not calculated ahead of time. Let sentence flow on sentence, no matter how nonsensical.

Open a book and read the first few paragraphs aloud. Close the book and decide what you would write next. Where does your own stock of images and experiences carry you?

Write a narrative with another person by writing alternate paragraphs and allowing the other person's paragraphs to stimulate yours.

Write nonsense. See if it makes sense. Write sense that is really nonsense.

If all else fails, go to bed. Perhaps you will have a dream or a nightmare that can serve as the inspirational center of your writing.

If you have been forced for a long time to extinguish the personal in your writing, it might be difficult to find your voice. Try some of these experiments in which you let yourself go:

Experiment with free association and stream of consciousness writing. Pick a starting point—an idea, issue, problem, or experience—and let the language flow in your own natural voice. How does this private voice differ from the one you put on in public?

Write a personal account in language you would use in talking with a close friend, of one of the following experiences (perhaps you have just called him or her on the phone):

a) an examination that you flubbed because . . .

b) a date that turned out to be dull because . . .

c) a surprise gift for a special friend because . . .

Write a batch of personal letters this weekend. (You're probably behind in your correspondence anyway.) Let your personal voice come through. Revel in writing about what you know best—your own thoughts, experiences, ideas, and feelings.

FURTHER POINTS OF DEPARTURE

A diary is simply a record of actions; but a journal is concerned with *re*actions—yours. Start a writing journal in which you can keep a record of reactions and responses to events in your life, experiment with writing, and search for your own voice and style. Use the journal to try a poem, to test out a writing voice, to explore a thought, to assess an experience.

In your journal, set aside a section labeled "The Rhetoric of the Imagination" for a running record of your encounter with words in the world. Jot down ideas for writing, for this course and others. Keep an account of one or several writing projects, including details about how you begin, where the flow of ideas carries you, and so on. Write down the pleasures and pains you experience. Use this journal to explore who you are as a writer and to note the progress that you make in coming months.

Collect samples of the work of a few writers whose writing seems to you especially good—novelists, poets, newspaper columnists. How do you characterize their voices? To what extent does their writing strike you as personal?

2
Public writing

James Britton has remarked, "Men make some things to serve a purpose, other things simply to please themselves."[1] In saying this, he touches on the two major kinds of writing in which people engage—private and public. Our private writing is done not so much to be shared with another person as to help us work out, confirm, or shape our thoughts and beliefs, to discover our identity, and to please ourselves.

Although public writing is primarily intended to inform or persuade others, it can be important in helping a writer understand himself. Public writing provides information, shares experiences, or creates an aesthetic experience in another person. It is of importance to individual writers, because it provides contact with the outside world, allowing them to confirm their sense of what is real and of what matters.

Of course any person using this book is necessarily concerned with the practical uses of language. While exploring and knowing the self through writing is important, there are day-to-day demands on our use of language and writing, demands that must be met if we are to survive in school and society. There are examinations and papers to be written, memos and letters, applications for school or jobs, speeches, essays, reviews, petitions, and so on.

In *Writing in Reality*, we will not talk about the form of the term paper or provide advice about writing examinations, applica-

[1] "Response to Literature," National Council of Teachers of English, 1968.

tions, or literary criticism. The forms of public writing are not set and firm although textbooks on writing have often deluded students into believing they are by providing rules and structures, by demanding formal outlines before one writes, and so on. The fact is that "the essay" is practically indefinable as a form. An essay can be anything from the humorous writing of a James Thurber to the formal report of a presidential commission to whatever it takes to get an "A" out of Professor Sirius in the Astronomy Department. (One of us once took courses in Victorian and Romantic literature the same term. One course was taught by an orderly chap who numbered the points in his lectures and expected the students to do the same in their papers, the other, by a rambler who loathed structured prose and would cry, "Don't give me your damned *conclusions,* let me see your *mind* at work!" No amount of instruction in the form of the essay could ease the pain of taking back-to-back final examinations in those two courses.)

Form in language grows from content—something the writer has to say—and that something, in turn, comes directly from the self. Writers who have nothing to say—be it about literary manners in Victorian England, amino acid interface chemistry, or their own loves and hates—will write formless prose, no matter how thorough their training in outlines and sentence structure (or in techniques of versification) has been.

Further, because writing is a process of exploration, one cannot always know what will emerge. Carl Jung describes this phenomenon: A writer who is following a plan and keeping within it suddenly goes off in a new, unexpected direction. The writer's mind seems almost to have developed a life and will of its own, and he or she looks with amazement on what has been written.

> There are many reasons why we forget things that we have noticed or experienced; and there are just as many ways in which they may be recalled to mind. An interesting example is that of cryptomnesia, or "concealed recollection." An author may be writing steadily to a preconceived plan, working out an argument or developing the line of a story, when he suddenly runs off at a tangent. Perhaps a fresh idea has occurred to him, or a

> different image, or a whole new sub-
> plot. If you ask him what prompted
> the digression, he will not be able
> to tell you. He may not even have
> noticed the change, though he has now
> produced material that is entirely
> fresh and apparently unknown to him
> before. Yet it can sometimes be shown
> convincingly that what he has written
> bears a striking similarity to the
> work of another author—a work that he
> believes he has never seen.
>
> CARL G. JUNG, *Man and His Symbols*

While your own tangents may never have been as extreme as the ones described by Jung, you have probably had similar experiences of starting to say one thing but winding up by saying quite another. Or you may have had the equally exciting experience of gaining a totally fresh insight while pursuing what you thought was a cut-and-dried topic. How does this happen? The human mind works in mysterious ways, and it is often difficult to figure out what it is up to. It seems understandable that a writer may start from one point of view but, by thinking and rethinking, stir his or her ideas enough to generate another point of view, which is more attractive and more persuasive.

Given the great variability of form in writing, it is surprising and regrettable that so much misdirected advice about organizing has been passed on from generation to generation. Take, for example, the platitudes and regulations which surround the planning of a paper. While it is obvious that some planning must be involved in any writing, advice such as "always outline before you write" is often singularly unhelpful to a writer. As many writers have exclaimed, "How do I know what I am going to write until I write it?" Notes on scraps of paper or shirt cuffs may help, but good writing cannot be preplanned like a vacation trip, especially within the confines of the formal outline. (A common solution to high school outlining assignments is one you may have tried: You write the full essay first and develop the outline later.)

We feel that the best preparation for the demands of practical writing is not just the writing of essays and research papers but experimenting with a wide range of the forms of public writing: writing about the world you observe and the world you would like to create, in narrative or drama, in propaganda or diatribe. One can say some kinds of things much more effectively in a poem than in an essay; a short story delivers a message in a very different way than does a one-act play. Too often writers fail to consider the wide range of public forms that are available for communicating their messages.

The possibilities are well worth exploring. For instance, it may be that you want to write about a deeply moving personal experience, something that influenced you powerfully. Perhaps you are far enough removed from the experience to write about it in the form of a first-person narrative. But the memories of the experience may be too strong, too powerful, too close for you to spill out in the first-person form; you might find it considerably more comfortable to use the short story for detachment—fictionalizing the experience to gain some distance from it. (Although reasons for the choice may differ, obviously a good many writers find fiction a useful way of presenting personal experiences.) Perhaps a poem—a piece of free verse—would allow you to present the emotion itself without the necessity of describing the details of the experience.

In another vein, if there is a public issue about which you feel strongly, you may want to write an essay setting out your opinion, and in some circumstances that will be quite effective. But as politicians and public relations people have long since discovered, there are a *variety* of forms that can be explored (or exploited) to publicize an idea: press releases, posters, "white" papers, advertisements, press conferences, editorials, television commercials, and so on. Experimenting with as many different forms as possible is critical and is valuable preparation for the demands of practical discourse. Even though some of the writing that we do is not especially creative—writing away for a spare part, notifying the telephone company of a mistake in its bill—much of the day-to-day writing in which we engage provides opportunity for genuine exploration and learning—discovering and rediscovering things about ourselves and our universe. A midterm examination, though threatening, provides opportunities for creative synthesis of what one has been learning, thinking, and feeling, as does a research paper, essay, or report.

DISCUSSION

In retrospect, observe yourself in argument, debate, or intense discussion. What did you say/do/contribute? How did your ideas build on the ideas of others? What new thoughts did you discover in yourself? Where and how did you find the language to express them?

Recall an important insight that came to you unsummoned. Reconstruct the incident with as much detail as you can recall, exploring the circumstances that may have brought about the insight.

Have you ever been surprised by what you have written? Have you ever changed your mind in the middle of writing an opinion about some matter? Explore the reasons this happened in your own case.

What works for you in writing for college courses? What techniques and strategies have you developed to make the writing go more smoothly?

WRITING IDEAS AND EXPERIMENTS

When writing "goes public" and one needs to be concerned about reaching his or her audience—the readership—successfully, revision becomes important. Revision, assuredly, is far more than proofreading for errors in spelling, punctuation, and usage. It may be that on your first draft you "hit it," discovering the flow of ideas you wanted, and revision requires only modest adjustments. At other times you may feel that it is not at all what you meant. Select one of the topics that follow and write for the public something you will share—with one other person, or with several people, or with a larger group. Begin to discover your own habits and patterns for revising. Experiment with one or several of the following:

Write a set of instructions on:
a) how to get from here to there.
b) how to do something (e.g., change a tire, change a diaper, change a mind).

Write the opening dialogue of a movie in which you are the star.

Write a story using:
a name you pick from the telephone book.
an episode from your childhood.

Create in words on paper:
a daydream.
an unreal world.
a better real world.

Write a serious or satirical description of someone from your past: teacher, friend, enemy, acquaintance.

Tell about the first time you fell in love or the last time you fell out of love.

Begin an essay with the most outrageous opinion you can invent that is not so far from the truth as to be unbelievable. Then show how you sometimes believe part of what you have just expressed. You will have to tease the reader a little along the way.

If you had ten minutes with the president (of the company, college, or country), what would you tell him or her? Make a set of notes or draft some of your comments.

Write a commercial for, or a diatribe attacking, your college or university.

FURTHER POINTS OF DEPARTURE

Here is a list of writing forms that are seldom used in school and college writing classes yet offer exciting possibilities for exploring your personal voice. Even though you may not have had much experience with some of these forms, try your hand at many of them, perhaps using your writer's journal as a place for experimentation.

Observation papers
Profiles and portraits
Sketches (thumbnail sketches, jottings)
Reminiscence
Memoir
Autobiography
Confession
Dramatic monologue
Scripts
Stream of consciousness
Satire
Children's stories or verse
Newspaper stories
Poetry (free forms and structured forms, rhymed and unrhymed, haiku, sonnet, concrete poetry, light verse, doggerel, epic)

Fiction
Light essays
Plays
Advertisements
Riddles
Posters
Flyers
Telegrams
Letters
Reviews
Feature essays
Interviews
Policy papers
Pamphlets
Petitions

As you experiment with new forms, keep rough notes on your experiences, to discuss with other people. Which forms fit best for you, allowing you to say what you have to say most effectively? Share your writing with other people and get their reactions. How do people respond differently to different forms?[2]

Explore ways of saying the same thing in different forms and media. How can you say "I love you" in poem, song, essay, letter, telegram, or even in painting or film?

In your writing journal, begin keeping a record of public reaction to what your write. How well are you succeeding at reaching your audience?

[2] A note on form: You may be reluctant to try some of these forms because you have never consciously thought about or studied them. We suggest, however, that you probably know more than you think you do, since you have been immersed in most of these print forms since first grade (or even earlier).

The creation
of the self

Thirteen's no age at all.   Thirteen is
   nothing.
It is not wit, or powder on the face,
Or Wednesday matinees, or misses'
   clothing.
Or intellect, or grace.
Twelve has its tribal customs.   But
   thirteen
Is neither boys in battered cars nor
   dolls,
Nor Sara Crewe or movie magazines,
Or pennants on the walls.

Thirteen keeps diaries and tropical
   fish
(A month, at most); scorns jumpropes
   in the spring;
Could not, would fortune grant it,
   name its wish;
Wants nothing, everything;
Has secrets from itself; friends it
   despises;
Admits none of the terrors that it
   feels;
Owns a half a hundred masks but no
   disguises;
And walks upon its heels.

Thirteen's anomalous—not that, not
   this:
Not folded bud, or wave that laps a
   shore,

Or moth proverbial from the chrysalis.
Is the one age defeats the metaphor.
Is not a town, like childhood, strongly
  walled
But easily surrounded; is not city.
Nor, quitted once, can it be quite
  recalled—
Not even with pity.

                              PHYLLIS MC GINLEY
              "Portrait of a Girl with a Comic Book," *Times Three*

South of the bridge on Seventeenth
I found back of the willows one summer
day a motorcycle with engine running
as it lay on its side, ticking over
slowly in the high grass. I was
  fifteen.

I admired all that pulsing gleam, the
shiny flanks, the demure headlights
fringed where it lay; I led it gently
to the road and stood with that
companion, ready and friendly. I was
  fifteen.

We could find the end of a road, meet
the sky out Seventeenth. I thought
  about
hills, and patting the handle got
  back a
confident opinion. On the bridge we
  indulged
a forward feeling, a tremble. I was
  fifteen.

Thinking, back farther in the grass I
  found
the owner, just coming to, where he
  had flipped
over the rail. He had blood on his
  hand, was pale—
I helped him walk to his machine. He
  ran his hand
over it, called me good man, roared away.

I stood there, fifteen.

              WILLIAM STAFFORD, "Fifteen," *The Rescued Year*

> Most of the basic material a writer
> works with is acquired before the age
> fifteen.
>
> WILLA CATHER, quoted in *Willa Cather* by René Rapin

> I think; therefore, I am.
>
> DESCARTES

Descartes' famous assertion might be modified slightly to suggest the ways experience and personality are deeply bound up with language: *I speak; therefore, I am.* We use language both to clarify experience for ourselves and to share it with other people. We literally establish our individuality, our distinctiveness as human beings, through language.

This process is complex, but it begins with a potential for language acquisition and language use that appears to be granted us as a birthright. The accident of birth will determine whether a child will speak Chinese, Swahili, Spanish, or English, and a similar accident will determine the kind of dialect he or she will acquire within that language. Yet most children go through a common process of learning how to use language. They are usually in an environment that is sympathetic to them and their growth, with mothers and family who encourage them to express themselves and to respond to events and experience. The baby babbles and it receives food and love; it utters a word, then several, and sees that the world responds; and finally, the child begins stringing words into sentences, sentences into discourse, and in an astonishingly short period of time—three to four years—has mastered most of the conventions of Chinese or Swahili or Spanish or English.

During the same period, the environment provides the baby with a rich range of experiences—being held and talked to, seeing cats and puppy dogs, falling off things, feeling pleasure and pain. At first these experiences are a kaleidoscopic blur, undiscriminated by the infant, but gradually events and objects assume shape and take on a recognizable consistency; the child begins using words to label the things that his or her senses perceive and, simultaneously, uses his or her growing language in an attempt to control the environment.

Language and experience continue to intermingle throughout our lives. Bombarded by sights and sounds, we use language to label and categorize our impressions. Puzzled and intrigued by

experiences, we use language internally—talking to ourselves—
to sort through and clarify what we think and feel. Driven to
make contact with other people and to exert a degree of control
over our experiences, we use language to communicate ideas, to
test out perceptions, to talk of what we know and do not know,
of fear, love, hate, wishes, and dreams. We speak; therefore,
we are.

> Who am I?
> As a bird I fly about,
> I sing of flowers;
> I compose songs,
> Butterflies of song.
> Let them burst forth from my soul!
> Let my heart be delighted with them!
>
> Aztec Teaching Poem

Because writing forces us to capture, retrieve, and bring into
focus stray and random thoughts, myriad ideas and experiences,
the writer must live an aware life. Sifting through our thoughts,
we make decisions that are as much about the self as they are
about language. In this way, writing that is honest and genuine
and serious (though not necessarily without humor or wit) con-
stitutes the discovery of the self.

> Whether we are drowning Japanese
> beetles in turpentine, or gathering
> seashells by the seashore, or having
> root-canal work done, or drinking up
> a storm at a cocktail party, we are
> at work as writers. We are eaves-
> dropping and spying and asking
> questions and stowing away the answers
> like pack rats.
>
> JEAN STAFFORD, *Saturday Review/World*

In setting forth on this voyage of self-discovery, it is best to
begin not with the problems of the universe, but with what sometimes appear to be the trivia of everyday life, large and small episodes and events from present or past. The self-examination
which occurs in simply writing an account of one's life for a
single day can bring unexpected illumination. Writing such an

account frees one to review and relive imaginatively moments of pain and fun, joy and sobriety. Events leave some kind of mark —intellectual, emotional, imaginative. What kind of mark? how deep? how long lasting? There are public events and private events—events for which there were some, perhaps many, witnesses, and events that had no witnesses at all.

All these events mark the individual's personal turf, providing material for his or her intellectual and imaginative use and growth. This belongs to one person alone, impossible to share totally with anyone else, no matter how close. It is the starting point for writing. A person who begins to feel the preciousness of this material, this segment of life that is his or her own and no one else's, is in fact feeling a sense of the self. As he or she discovers sequence and significance in the events—large and small —the individual is making the discovery of self that the process of writing can bring about

Mark Twain skillfully and artistically resurrects a series of events and feelings from his youth to explore the creation of his *self*.

So by and by I ran away. I said I never would come home again until I was a [steamboat] pilot and could come in glory. . . . I packed my valise, and took passage on an ancient tub called the Paul Jones, for New Orleans. For the sum of sixteen dollars I had the scarred and tarnished splendors of "her" main saloon principally to myself, for she was not a creature to attract the eye of wiser travellers.

When we presently got under way and went poking down the broad Ohio from Cincinnati, I became a new being, and the subject of my own admiration. I was a traveller! A word had never tasted so good in my mouth before. I had an exultant sense of being bound for mysterious lands and distant climes which I never have felt in so uplifting a degree since. I was in such a glorified condition that all ignoble feelings departed out of me, and I was able to look down and pity the untravelled with a compassion that had hardly a trace of contempt in it. Still, when we stopped at villages and wood-yards, I could not help lolling carelessly upon the railings of the boiler deck to enjoy the envy of the country boys on the bank. If they did not seem to discover me, I presently sneezed to attract their attention, or moved to a position where they could not help seeing me. And as soon as I knew they saw me I gaped and stretched, and gave other signs of being mightily bored with travelling.

I kept my cap off all the time, and stayed where the wind and the sun could strike me, because I wanted to get the bronzed and weather-beaten look of an old traveller. Before the second day was half gone, I experienced a joy which filled me with the purest gratitude; for I saw that the skin had begun to blister and peel off my face and neck. I wished that the boys and girls at home could see me now.

We reached Louisville in time—at least the neighborhood of it. We stuck hard and fast on the rocks in the middle of the river and lay there four days. I was now beginning to feel a strong sense of being a part of the boat's family, a sort of infant son to the captain and younger brother to the officers. There is no estimating the pride I took in this grandeur, or the affection that began to swell and grow in me for those people. I could not know how the lordly steamboatman scorns that sort of presumption in a mere landsman. I particularly longed to acquire the least trifle of notice from the big stormy mate, and I was on the alert for an opportunity to do him a service to that end. It came at last. The riotous powwow of setting a spar was going on down on the forecastle, and I went down there and stood around in the way—or mostly skipping out of it—till the mate suddenly roared a general order for somebody to bring him a capstan bar. I sprang to his side and said: "Tell me where it is—I'll fetch it!"

If a rag-picker had offered to do a diplomatic service for the Emperor of Russia, the monarch could not have been more astounded than the mate was. He even stopped swearing. He stood and stared down at me. It took him ten seconds to scrape his disjointed remains together again. Then he said impressively: "Well, if this don't beat hell!" and turned to his work with the air of a man who had been confronted with a problem too abstruse for solution.

I crept away, and courted solitude for the rest of the day. I did not go to dinner; I stayed away from supper until everybody else had finished. I did not feel so much like a member of the boat's family now as before. However, my spirits returned, in installments, as we pursued our way down the river. I was sorry I hated the mate so, because it was not in (young) human nature not to admire him. He was huge and muscular, his face was bearded and whiskered all over; he had a red woman and a blue woman tattooed on his right arm,—one on each side of a blue anchor with a red rope to it; and in the matter of profanity he was perfect. When he was getting out cargo at a landing, I was always where I could see and hear. He felt all the sublimity of his great position, and made the world feel it, too. When he gave even the simplest order, he discharged it like a blast of lightning, and sent a long, reverberating peal of profanity thundering after it. I could not help contrasting the way in which the average landsman would give an order, with the mate's way of doing it. If the landsman should wish the gangplank moved a foot farther forward, he would probably say: "James, or William, one of you push that plank forward, please;" but put the mate in his place, and he would roar out: "Here, now, start that gang-plank for'ard! Lively, now. *What're* you about! Snatch it! *snatch* it! There! there! Aft again! aft again! Don't you hear me? Dash it to dash! are you going to *sleep* over it! *'Vast* heaving. 'Vast heaving, I tell you! Going to heave it clear

astern? WHERE're you going with the barrel! *for'ard* with it 'fore
I make you swallow it, you dash-dash-dash-*dashed* split between a
tired mud-turtle and a crippled hearsehorse!"

I wished I could talk like that.

MARK TWAIN, "Old Times on the Mississippi"

In addition to showing some of the ways in which language
and experience are intertwined, Twain's narrative suggests another aspect of language and personal growth: the kind of testing
processes in which people—particularly young people—engage.
We project visions of an imagined reality, visions of a world we
anticipate, desire, or admire, and test those visions against our
experience. In that way we sharpen those visions and, in the process, our sense of reality and sense of self.

DISCUSSION

Willa Cather remarked, "Most of the basic material a writer works
with is acquired before the age of fifteen." Consider the meaning of that statement in view of your own experience. Does
it mean that there is no life after fifteen? To what extent do
your childhood and adolescent experiences establish a pattern
of perceiving (and using language) that becomes fixed?

What can people write about after the age of fifteen? Discuss this
advice offered by Henry James:

Oh, do something from your point of view; an ounce of example
is worth a ton of generalities . . . do something with life. Any
point of view is interesting that is a direct impression of life.
You each have an impression colored by your individual
conditions; make that into a picture, a picture framed by your
own personal wisdom, your glimpse of the American world.
The field is vast for freedom, for study, for observation, for satire,
for truth.

In the rush of modern life, many people spend most of their time
thinking of what they have just done and what they plan to
do next rather than savoring the moment. To what extent is
this true (or not true) of you? Spend some time resurrecting
key moments of the past day or two. Are you aware of what
is happening in the way Jean Stafford suggests?

Everybody goes through a series of philosophies in the process of
growing up. At stages people believe they have figured everything out; but then the belief is undermined, a crisis follows,

and the painful process of constructing another belief is repeated. With several other people with whom you feel comfortable, look over your life and discuss the stages of your beliefs and the crises that changed them.

WRITING IDEAS AND EXPERIMENTS

Mark Twain's story triggers strong responses in many readers because most of us have had similar experiences or feelings at one time or another—the romance of imagining far-off places, the aching desire to be grown up, or even the dream of "lighting out" to escape the environment that helped to create us. Dip back into your own memory and try to capture one of those experiences in a personal narrative like Twain's. Or write a poem or short story that deals with the experience. As a follow-up, jot down some notes indicating how you think this episode influenced you.

Phyllis McGinley's "Portrait of a Girl with a Comic Book" captures another feeling experienced by most young people—a moment of non-identity, a time of simply not knowing who one is or what will happen next. If you can recall such a moment from childhood, write about it in narrative, stream of consciousness, or even poem.

William Stafford's "Fifteen" describes a different moment, an instant of communication and insight, a moment when a young person makes contact with the adult world and has a sense of satisfaction and well-being. It is a stage beyond Twain's wistful admiration of the steamboat mate. Try to capture such a moment in your own life.

"The writer, when he sits down to commerce, should do so not because he has to tell a story, but because he has a story to tell."
ANTHONY TROLLOPE

What are the stories that you have to tell? Pick one from your past and tell it, noting how the language flows when you have a good tale to spin.

Recapture feelings of childhood by writing a children's story (or some children's verse) that would have delighted you as a child.

Explore the nature of a small event that appeared big to you in the way it turned, or seemed to turn, the course of your life.

Give an imaginative account of the affect of the event on others on the periphery of it—those whom it touched but did not similarly move.

FURTHER POINTS OF DEPARTURE

Make an outline of your autobiography. List the key episodes and incidents of your life. Which of these events deserve treatment in whole chapters? What are the specific episodes that were crucial in the creation of the self? In coming weeks and months, write some of those chapters.

Because many people have been taught to feel they are inadequate writers, they have also developed a sense of despair over finding things to write about. Yet, every human being has a rich storehouse of ideas, experiences, dreams, and visions. Below are several categories of ideas and experiences. Go through the list and jot down ideas from your own experience on each topic, realizing that every idea you list is a valid and legitimate starting point for writing. As you proceed through this book, draw on your list.

Reminiscences. (Fond and not-so-fond memories from the near and distant past)

Stories, tales, anecdotes. (From your own experience, or stories you create)

Animosities and aggressions. (Yours and others)

Ambitions and hopes.

Doubts. (About self, about others)

Wildly improbable schemes and visions.

People, places, things.

Television/film/music.

Dreams and fantasies.

Public issues and problems.

You can probably come up with a half-dozen ideas for each category and, in all probability, develop a dozen more categories. Don't forget things like living and dying, emotions, sin, human relationships, conversations, gossip, dares, and adventures. . . .

In your "Rhetoric of the Imagination" spend a page or two writing about the effect reminiscing has on you. As you uncover forgotten episodes and moments, how does your perspective on the present change?

Versions
of the self

> I was trying to write . . . and I
> found the greatest difficulty, aside
> from knowing truly what you really
> felt, rather than what you were sup-
> posed to feel, and had been taught to
> feel, was to put down what really
> happened in action; what the actual
> things were which produced the emotion
> that you experienced. In writing for
> a newspaper you told what happened
> and, with one trick or another, you
> communicated the emotion aided by the
> element of timeliness which gives a
> certain emotion to any account of
> something that has happened on that
> day; but the real thing, the sequence
> of motion and fact which made the
> emotion and which would be as valid in
> a year or in ten years or, with luck
> and if you stated it purely enough,
> always, was beyond me and I was work-
> ing very hard to try to get it.
>
> ERNEST HEMINGWAY, *Death in the Afternoon*

When you begin a serious examination of your own life, questions and problems that you may have put away without facing
directly begin to surface. We tend to understand least what we
live with daily and intimately; to know oneself—exploring the
darkest and most distant corners of the mind—requires great will
and effort and keen imagination. Whitman has put the matter
very well in a short poem, "When I Read the Book":

When I read the book, the biography famous,
And is this then (said I) what the author calls a man's life?
And so will some one when I am dead and gone write my life?
    (As if any man really knew aught of my life),
Why even I myself I often think know little or nothing of my real life,
Only a few hints, a few diffuse faint clews and indirections
I seek for my own use to trace out here.

We all, like Whitman, have a real life within, which parallels but is by no means identical to our exterior life. And it is probably true that if Whitman knew "little or nothing" of his real life, we know little of ours. If we are to come to know it, as we probably would like, we must follow the "few hints," the "few diffuse faint clews and indirections" that we find.

> For some time now—I think since I was
> a child—I have been possessed of the
> desire to put down the stuff of my
> life. That is a commonplace impulse,
> apparently, among persons of massive
> self-interest; sooner or later we all
> do it. And, I am quite certain, there
> is only one internal quarrel: How
> much of the truth to tell: How much,
> how much, how much! It is brutal, in
> sober uncompromising moments, to
> reflect on the comedy of concern we
> all enact when it comes to our precious
> images!
> LORRAINE HANSBERRY, *To Be Young, Gifted, and Black*

There are no doubt many reasons for the difficulty in attaining self-knowledge, but one of the most common is the unconscious suppression of the self. People are expected to feel certain kinds of emotions on certain kinds of occasions, and they develop the habit of expressing those emotions whether they feel them or not. Indeed, our habits often muddle up our feelings so that we are unable to sort through them to know just how we do feel. In the following autobiographical passage, the poet Langston Hughes describes a moment in his life when he was pressured by outsiders to see and feel and believe and say things that were not there for him, were not true for him:

I was saved from sin when I was going on thirteen. But not really saved. It happened like this. There was a big revival at my Auntie Reed's church. Every night for weeks there had been much preaching, singing, praying, and shouting, and some very hardened sinners had been brought to Christ, and the membership of the church had grown by leaps and bounds. Then just before the revival ended, they held a special meeting for children, "to bring the young lambs to the fold." My aunt spoke of it for days ahead. That night I was escorted to the front row and placed on the mourners' bench with all the other young sinners, who had not yet been brought to Jesus.

My aunt told me that when you were saved you saw a light, and something happened to you inside! And Jesus came into your life! And God was with you from then on! She said you could see and hear and feel Jesus in your soul. I believed her. I had heard a great many old people say the same thing and it seemed to me they ought to know. So I sat there calmly in the hot, crowded church, waiting for Jesus to come to me.

The preacher preached a wonderful rhythmical sermon, all moans and shouts and lonely cries and dire pictures of hell, and then he sang a song about the ninety and nine safe in the fold, but one little lamb was left out in the cold. Then he said: "Won't you come? Won't you come to Jesus? Young lambs, won't you come?" And he held out his arms to all of us young sinners there on the mourners' bench. And the little girls cried. And some of them jumped up and went to Jesus right away. But most of us just sat there.

A great many old people came and knelt around us and prayed, old women with jet-black faces and braided hair, old men with work-gnarled hands. And the church sang a song about the lower lights are burning, some poor sinners to be saved. And the whole building rocked with prayer and song.

Still I kept waiting to *see* Jesus.

Finally all the young people had gone to the altar and were saved, but one boy and me. He was a rounder's son named Westley. Westley and I were surrounded by sisters and deacons praying. It was very hot in the church, and getting late now. Finally Westley said to me in a whisper: "Oh, god. Oh, damn! I'm tired o' sitting here. Let's get up and be saved." So he got up and was saved.

Then I was left all alone on the mourners' bench. My aunt came and knelt at my knees and cried, while prayers and songs swirled all around me in the little church. The whole congregation prayed for me alone, in a mighty wail of moans and voices. And I kept waiting serenely for Jesus, waiting, waiting—but he didn't come. I wanted to see him, but nothing happened to me. Nothing! I wanted something to happen to me, but nothing happened.

I heard the songs and the minister saying: "Why don't you come? My dear child, why don't you come to Jesus? Jesus is waiting for you. He wants you. Why don't you come? Sister Reed, what is this child's name?"

"Langston," my aunt sobbed.

"Langston, why don't you come? Why don't you come and be saved? Oh, Lamb of God! Why don't you come?"

Now it was really getting late. I began to be ashamed of myself, holding everything up so long. I began to wonder what God thought about Westley, who certainly hadn't seen Jesus either, but who was now sitting proudly on the platform, swinging his knickerbockered legs and grinning down at me, surrounded by deacons and old women on their knees praying. God had not struck Westley dead for taking his name in vain or for lying in the temple. So I decided that maybe to save further trouble, I'd better lie, too, and say that Jesus had come, and get up and be saved.

So I got up.

Suddenly the whole room broke into a sea of shouting, as they saw me rise. Waves of rejoicing swept the place. Women leaped in the air. My aunt threw her arms around me. The minister took me by the hand and led me to the platform.

When things quieted down, in a hushed silence, punctuated by a few ecstatic "Amens," all the new young lambs were blessed in the name of God. Then joyous singing filled the room.

That night, for the last time in my life but one—for I was a big boy twelve years old—I cried. I cried, in bed alone, and couldn't stop. I buried my head under the quilts, but my aunt heard me. She woke up and told my uncle I was crying because the Holy Ghost had come into my life, and because I had seen Jesus. But I was really crying because I couldn't bear to tell her that I had lied, that I had deceived everybody in the church, and I hadn't seen Jesus, and that now I didn't believe there was a Jesus any more, since he didn't come to help me.

LANGSTON HUGHES, *The Big Sea*

Despite the fact that he faked seeing Jesus, Hughes remained true to himself in this episode. However, his crying at night gives indication of the strain the external pressures had placed on him. While not all pressures not to be oneself are as overt as those placed on young Langston, we feel and experience similar strain daily. In fact, many of us have become so conditioned to hiding or suppressing our feelings that we can no longer find those that are really there, down deep below the ones that we pretend to have because society demands them. It is possible that even if we can free ourselves from exterior demands and pressures, we may still find ourselves confronted with a number of possibilities and unable to choose among them because we are uncertain who and what we are or want to be. We can, in short, be several selves or none or one.

> Each man's life represents a road
> toward himself, an attempt at such a
> road, the intimation of a path. No
> man has ever been entirely and com-
> pletely himself. Yet each one strives
> to become that—one in an awkward, the
> other in a more intelligent way, each
> as best he can. Each man carries the
> vestiges of his birth—the slime and
> eggshells of his primeval past—with
> him to the end of his days. Some
> never become human, remaining frog,
> lizard, ant. Some are human above the
> waist, fish below. Each represents a
> gamble on the part of nature in creation
> of the human. We all share the same
> origin, our mothers; all of us come in
> at the same door. But each of us—
> experiments of the depths—strives
> toward his own destiny. We can
> understand one another; but each of us
> is able to interpret himself to
> himself alone.
>
> HERMANN HESSE, *Demian*

The self deserves intimate acquaintance, even when it presents several sides, all puzzling. For the struggling writer in search of sentences, this elusive, interior self presents some of the best material—and certainly the most exclusive—because it is inaccessible to anybody else. As Ernest Hemingway pointed out, one of the great problems is to "know what you truly felt, rather than what you were supposed to feel."

Where and what is the role of the self in the process of writing? It is clearly no easy task to follow the injunction to "let the self go on paper." What self? which self? how many selves? There are some choices to be made. Most well-known writers seem to have found a single self, a single voice and used it in their work. A glance at two passages, one from Emily Dickinson and one from Walt Whitman can leave no doubt which lines belong to which poet:

I'm Nobody! Who are you?
Are you—Nobody—Too?
Then there's a pair of us!
Don't tell! they'd banish us—you know!

How dreary—to be—Somebody!
How public—like a Frog—
To tell your name—the livelong June—
To an admiring Bog!

*   *   *

Walt Whitman, a kosmos, of Manhattan the son,
Turbulent, fleshy, sensual, eating, drinking and breeding,
No sentimentalist, no stander above men and women or apart
      from them,
No more modest than immodest.

Unscrew the locks from the doors!
Unscrew the doors themselves from their jambs!

Whoever degrades another degrades me,
And whatever is done or said returns at last to me.

Even without Whitman's name in his poem, and even without wide acquaintance with their poetry, it is not a difficult task to assign the right lines to Whitman and Dickinson. It seems absurd to us now that one critic, back in the nineteenth century, advised Emily Dickinson to become the female Walt Whitman. She was clearly incapable of assuming the expansive and aggressive voice that marks Whitman's every line; and he was as incapable of writing in her coy, yet restrained, voice.

Although Dickinson cannot be Whitman, nor Whitman, Dickinson, it is still true that we have some choice in the selection of self in our writing, choice of the tone and color of the voice with which we speak. Just as we assume many roles in our lives—one in our family, another in the classroom, still another in a dormitory, another on the job, and many more—so we are able to speak in many different voices, ranging through several degrees of formality. If we gossip with a friend, we speak in a tone of voice that would be inappropriate for delivering a eulogy at a funeral. The tone at the funeral would be incongruous in a classroom discussion; and the tone for the classroom would be jarring if used in a formal speech at a formal dinner.

But there is another, more important connection between the self and the voice used in various situations, for when you are fully and deeply in touch with your real self and your real feelings, it will be reflected in the tone and vigor of your writing. When people write from the self, their writing is better than when they are writing in a false voice from a false self. Conversely, much bad writing grows from the false selves in a person, from the "hollow" man.

DISCUSSION

Bring to class writing that you have done at various times in the past—papers, essays, letters, diaries, and the like. Analyze the selves and voices you see. Which seem most natural? Which least? What is the natural range of voices and selves which you present in your writing?

Try to describe the way the voice you use in private writing differs from the one you use when writing for others. What would be gained or lost if you used your private voice in public?

There have probably been many times in your life when you resisted the temptation and pressure to stifle your own voice. Recall an incident or two from childhood (or even adulthood) and discuss it and its effects on you.

Does it seem possible to fake a voice in writing? Can individuals write consistently from hollowness without being detected? Venture an opinion based on your own experience.

WRITING IDEAS AND EXPERIENCES

Oh wad some Pow'r the giftie gie us
To see oursels as others see us!
    ROBERT BURNS, "To a Louse"

Try your hand at seeing yourself as others see you. Do a multiple self-portrait of yourself as you think you appear to a number of others—your mother, your brother, your closest friend, your most hated enemy, your teacher, or anyone else who may have a clear image of you. You might want to set the record straight by concluding with a portrait of the real you.

Write an imaginary dialogue between two characters, both of them you, or a dialogue between you and your opposite.

Search for new voices and unexplored aspects of yourself. Look for, and write from, your arrogant self or proud self or meek self. Write from a self that is in love, or one filled with hate and contempt. Which feel comfortable to you? Which strain or inhibit you?

Choose one of the times when you were being pushed to be something or someone other than your real, your best self. Recount the episode in a personal narrative.

Explore the human relationships in your life. How many roles do you think you play? How many versions of yourself are you able to define? Write an essay in which you describe your various identities in your various roles. How does your use of language help you shape that role?

Every person contains a self that he or she would like to be. Write about that self—for yourself only. To what extent does the self you want to be, or wish you were, mesh with the true self that you know?

FURTHER POINTS OF DEPARTURE

The search for self is a common theme in literature. Below is a list of fictional and autobiographical accounts of coming of age.

Alex Kates Shulman, *Memoirs of an Ex-Prom Queen*
Maya Angelou, *I Know Why the Caged Bird Sings*
Hannah Green, *I Never Promised You a Rose Garden*
J. D. Salinger, *The Catcher in the Rye*
John Knowles, *A Separate Peace*
James Kirkwood, *Good Times, Bad Times*
Richard Wright, *Black Boy*
Richard Hughes, *A High Wind in Jamaica*
Piri Thomas, *Down These Mean Streets*
Sylvia Plath, *The Bell Jar*
Alex Haley, *Roots*
James T. Farrell, *Studs Lonigan*
Mark Twain, *Life on the Mississippi*
Claude Brown, *Manchild in the Promised Land*

It might be useful for you to read one or more longer works that deal with some of the kinds of experiences and emotions that you are sorting through in your own writing.

Keep a journal account of your response to the book(s) you chose, including answers to such questions as:

    a. What do you find you have in common with the central character in the book? What thoughts, feelings, concerns do you share?

    b. How does the character "work out" his or her true self (if, in fact, the character succeeds in doing so)?

    c. Are there episodes in the book that remind you of experiences in your younger days? How did your own experience differ?

5
How deep
can one go?

How deep, finally, can one go? Are there limits to the explorations of the self? barriers and depths one should not try to pass? We should surely probe to the level of biases, prejudices, hatreds, and hypocrisies; and perhaps to the fears beneath them. Normally we hide this darker self, even from ourselves. Of course, as part of the condition of being human, each of us has this nastier side, with inexplicable dislikes, blindnesses, hostilities. They flash out in our behavior, sometimes surprising even ourselves. But if we are able to come to terms with our fears and irrational feelings, we can participate more actively, directly, and consciously in that creation of the self which is the major challenge of existence.

Further, the deeper self is not necessarily the darker self. Murkiness is no more likely to be found there than brightness, and exploring the depths, one is likely to find positive aspects, too —an unexpected capacity for love, a suppressed compassion, a sense of humor that seldom surfaces. Sigmund Freud seemed to imply that the deeper self is a kind of sewer into which people dump all the unhealthy and nasty elements of the conscious mind; D. H. Lawrence believed that it includes a set of primitive impulses which can lead to purity and health; Carl Jung believed that it is both private and "collective," connecting ultimately with a "racial unconscious" (a kind of universal unconscious of all men who ever lived), which is the source of mankind's archetypal myths. Whatever its nature, the deeper self can be reached only through introspection.

Clad in this "self," the creation of
irresponsible and ignorant persons,
meaningless honors and catalogued acts
—strapped into the strait jacket of
the immediate.

To step out of all this, and stand
naked on the precipice of dawn—
acceptable, invulnerable, free: in the
Light, with the Light, of the Light.
Whole, real in the Whole.

Out of myself, as a stumbling block,
into myself as fulfillment.

                    DAG HAMMARSKJÖLD, *Markings*

In *Markings*, Dag Hammarskjöld presented—in language—
some of his own observations, the kinds of observations possible
only when one shakes off the demands of the outer self—"the
creation of irresponsible and ignorant persons, meaningless honors, and catalogued acts"—to make contact with the real "self":
"Out of myself as a stumbling block, into myself as fulfillment."
Yoga meditation is intended to teach the same thing, helping the
practitioner to still the buzzing of the ordinary, day-to-day mind
in order to allow him to be in tune with the universal. In several
religions, prayer is intended as a means of accomplishing the
same thing, and much of psychotherapy aims at this goal—allowing one to find the deeper self. Of course, such an organized
search is not imperative; most of us can probe deeply into the
self at moments of peace and tranquility—while walking in the
woods, doing laps in the pool, jogging, talking with friends,
reading.

Unconscious thinking, perceiving, or
communication is mythological, poetic,
metaphorical, preverbal, often concrete rather than conceptualized. It
is characteristic of our night and
day dreams, of our imagination, of
revery, of an essential aspect of all
art, of the first stages of creative
production, of free association, etc.
It is generally stigmatized by most
well-adjusted, sane, sober adults in
the West as childish, crazy, senseless,

```
wild.  It is thus threatening to their
adult adjustment to the outer world,
regarded as incompatible with it and
therefore often repudiated.  This
means it cannot be communicated with,
and cannot be used.
```
ABRAHAM H. MASLOW, *Sign, Image, Symbol*

Insights can also come indirectly, through dreams, fantasies, and reveries. Dreams have fascinated men from the beginning of time, in part because they remain basically fantastic and mysterious. The dream is, above all else, a private preserve. No one can truly possess another's dream. Even when possessed by the dreamer and held in the waking mind for examination, dreams frequently defy understanding. They seem to be made up of bizarre and incongruous elements, of fragments from various times, of encounters that would be impossible in real life. Dreams are filled with both terror and ecstasy. Most of us have experienced in our dreams the sensations of flying, of being pursued by a grotesque creature that threatened our lives, and of being caressed by a loving person who promised ultimate fulfillment. We have felt embarrassment at appearing nude in front of an audience, or triumph at bringing an audience to its feet in wild applause. We have had many experiences in our dreams that we have not, and perhaps never could have, had in real life.

Indeed, there is a surrealistic dimension in most dreams, with irrational juxtapositions, impossible events, unreal landscapes: a symbolism that teases one with its hidden meanings and messages. Fiction writers, who have found the dream a rich source, have frequently used the dream as a technique to represent symbolically the situations or dilemmas of their characters. In *The Victim,* Saul Bellow tells the dream of Aza Leventhal on one hot summer night in New York:

He slept but he did not rest. His heart beat swiftly and the emotions of the day still filled him. He had an unclear dream in which he held himself off like an unwilling spectator; yet it was he that did everything. He was in a railroad station, carrying a heavy suitcase, forcing his way with it through a crowd the sound of whose shuffling rose toward the flags hanging by the hundreds in the arches. He had missed his train, but the loudspeaker announced that a second section of it was leaving in three minutes. The gate was barely in sight; he could never reach it in time. There was a recoil of the crowd—the guards must have been pushing it back—and he found himself in a corridor

which was freshly paved and plastered. It seemed to lead down to
the tracks. "Maybe they've just opened this and I'm the first to find
it," he thought. He began to run and suddenly came to a barrier,
a movable frame resembling a sawhorse. Holding the suitcase before
him, he pushed it aside. Two men stopped him. "You can't go through,
I've got people working here," one of them said. He wore a business
suit and a fedora, and he looked like a contractor. The other man
was in overalls. "I must, I've got to get to the tracks," Leventhal said.
"There's a gate upstairs. This isn't open to the public. Didn't you see
the sign on the door? What door did you come through?" "I didn't
come through any door," said Leventhal angrily. "This is an emer-
gency; the train's leaving." The second man appeared to be a
thoughtful, sympathetic person, but he was an employee and couldn't
interfere. "You can't go back the way you came, either," the contractor
told him. "There's a sign up there. You'll have to leave through here."
Leventhal turned and a push on the shoulder sent him into an alley.
His face was covered with tears. A few people noticed this, but he
did not care about them.

SAUL BELLOW, *The Victim*

Although this dream has particular symbolic meaning for the
protagonist of Bellow's novel, it also has the ring of familiarity to
anyone who remembers his more frightening dreams—of seeking
a way out of a maze, of being pursued, of looking for exits and
entrances, or walking down endless corridors or tunnels, of falling through openings or from heights.

Unleashed from reason and detached
from circumstance, the play of dreams
is armed with terrible freedom. In
all history and every recorded culture
the mysterious and evanescent dream
has been taken seriously. Strategic
dream interpretations have altered the
course of nations, as did Joseph with
the fat kine and lean. Oracles dreamed
the future. By pagan dream-rites the
sick were healed. Lincoln's dream of
death seemed a harbinger of his fate.
American Indians enacted their dreams.
During the reign of terror and super-
stition from the 12th through the
17th century, Western Europeans fought
an international conspiracy of witches,
and the seriousness of the dream was
evident in the Malleus, guide and

handbook to every judge of the Inqui-
sition, at a time when dreams might
mean burning. Dreams also inspired
poetry in Coleridge, fiction in Robert
Louis Stevenson, and Kekule, the
organic chemist, is said to have
deciphered the arrangement of atoms
in the benzene ring by a dream of a
snake eating its tail. The skillful
man, said Emerson, reads his dreams
for self-knowledge. Although dream
books including codes for gamblers and
advice on all aspects of practical
life are abundant on newsstands today,
we tend to probe dreams for insight
into the dreamer.

Current Research on Dreams, Public
Health Service Publication No. 1389

Somewhat less mysterious and more comprehensible, but no less interesting for the insights they offer into the self, are "day" dreams—fantasy and reverie. Young children make productive use of daydreams, leading fantasy lives, engaging freely in dramatic play and reverie, living vicariously through literature, and this use of fantasy and daydream is important in the establishment of identity in the child.

However, as Abraham Maslow suggested in the epigraph presented earlier in this chapter, the indulgence in unconscious thinking that leads to daydreams is regarded (in Western culture, at least) as "childish, crazy, senseless, wild," and this is surely regrettable. Adults do daydream and fantasize regularly, but when fantasy is coupled with a sense of embarrassment, the adult frequently fails to realize the significance of the fantasy. Too often the wistful reverie is seen only as "wishful thinking," rather than as something growing directly from the self and deserving serious exploration.

Finally, it must be admitted that there are interior spaces that cannot be penetrated, where no light can shine, and where no individual can enter. These are the spaces of darkness and silence, of terror, of ecstasy, a mysterious province beyond our control and understanding.

The task of diving deep within oneself and finding what really lurks there is not an easy or comfortable one; nor can it ever be completely successful. Still it is important—even definitive—in the discovery of the self, and what will be uncovered cannot be predicted in advance. This introspection is a job for language— language that allows one to proceed in some kind of orderly fashion.

DISCUSSION

Have you ever had what you might call an encounter with your deepest self? Was it in some way mystical? Can you express what you learned from the encounter in words? Can you describe the circumstances of the experience?

Borrow a dream from a classmate or friend and work out an interpretation. What is the reaction of the dreamer to your interpretation? How does your interpretation compare to his or hers?

Make an exploration in depth of one of your prejudices, biases, or pet peeves. If you think you don't have any, think again. Dig into its roots and find out what you can of its hidden and deeper sources. Why does it grow and flourish? What might you do to eradicate it? Or do you think it is a virtue that should flourish?

WRITING IDEAS AND EXPERIMENTS

Begin an essay with the sentence: "I am the strangest character I know." Describe yourself as you think you really are, with all the depths that few people ever glimpse.

What evidence can you find within yourself that you do, or do not, have an unconscious? Write a serious (or comic) account of a person who discovers his or her unconscious, falls into it accidentally, or realizes suddenly that he or she does not have one.

Create an imaginary dream, for yourself or custom-written for someone else. Indulge yourself in creating fantastic landscapes, bizarre scenes, and impossible events.

Try casting one of your own dreams in the form of a poem or use your dream as the basis for a poem but, if you like, give more substance and form to the poem than the dream originally had.

Explore your own fantasy life by writing down a series of wishful thoughts or episodes in narrative or essay form. When you take these seriously, what insights do they offer into your surrealistic self?

Write a short story about an individual who appears to be trapped —physically or psychologically. Invent a dream or nightmare which represents his situation symbolically and work it into the story.

FURTHER POINTS OF DEPARTURE

Keep a diary of your dreams to discover whether any pattern emerges. Write an account and an interpretation.

Following is one from a whole book of "markings" that represents Hammarskjöld's gropings towards an understanding of basic, as opposed to superficial, values in life as it is lived:

> What I ask for is absurd: that life shall have a meaning.
> What I strive for is impossible: that my life shall acquire a meaning.
> I dare not believe, I do not see how I shall ever be able to believe:
> that I am not alone.
>
> DAG HAMMARSKJÖLD, *Markings*

Keep a book of "markings" in your journal, a series of deeper thoughts jotted down over a period of time as they occur. What are you able to discover about yourself—your real self —through your "markings"?

A number of authors have chosen to use fantasy as a literary form. Read one or two books from the Chronicles of Narnia, by C. S. Lewis (*The Lion, the Witch, and the Wardrobe*; *The Voyage of the "Dawn Treader"*; *The Magician's Nephew*), or explore the writings of J. R. R. Tolkien: *The Hobbitt* or The Lord of the Rings trilogy (*The Fellowship of the Ring, The Two Towers, The Return of the King*). How do these writers use fantasy and the surreal to probe real issues, problems, and concerns?

Encountering the world

As I lie here wondering
I feel an angry gust swish around my
    legs
The grass bustles about like a green
    jungle
The leaves flap about,
As paper whirls around the playground.
The seagulls squabble over scraps
And look greedily for more.
Little insects crawl through the grass
    jungle
Like wild animals.
In the small world I know little about
I lie here wondering.

KEVIN WINDSOR, age 9, "Wondering," from *Miracles*

Each self is the center of a universe. If we believe what our senses seem to tell us, the entire world is arranged around us to be apprehended by us. As we move, the circumference of our circle moves with us; we can never reach its edge. But as we move, the circle takes in new and different visions and experiences; our universe is constantly changing—developing, decaying, shifting, altering. Each day the world is a new world, waiting for us to rediscover it.

There remains the exhilaration of first discovery. When as children we first looked out onto the world, the excitement was difficult to contain. We began to possess the world by naming it, for as we learned a word for an object, it became ours. Many people continue to feel some sense of wonder as each day they walk out into the world—a world which presents views, sounds, odors, tastes, textures of infinite variety and grossness and subtlety. Others lose the exhilaration that comes with seeing the world afresh. Their senses brutalized or numbed, they drift through life oblivious to the sights and sounds which move in and out of their universe.

Writers have always tried to preserve their sense of wonder at the world. Many poets have hoped that part of the primary effect of their poetry would be wonder, awakening the excitement of their youth in readers. Here is part of Walt Whitman's, "There was a child went forth":

There was a child went forth every day,
And the first object he look'd upon, that object he became,
And that object became part of him for the day or a certain part
of the day,
Or for many years or stretching cycles of years

WALT WHITMAN, from "There was a child went forth."

Although Whitman is speaking in metaphor, we do in some sense "collect" the world as we move through it. We gather impressions and store them away inside, there to mingle with other memories and perceptions, to become an intimate part of us. Further, the impressions we collect shape the way we see and encounter the world—the past shapes the future. This collecting of the world goes on from the moment of entering it to the moment of departing from it. It is not peculiar to childhood, but children are generally more excited about the encounter, more delighted in gathering a great sweep of impressions, and more alive to, and conscious of, the impact it has on their lives and their interior being.

By learning to name things a child does not simply add a list of artificial signs to his previous knowledge of ready-made empirical objects. He learns rather to form the concepts of those objects, to come to terms with the objective world. . . . The first names of which a child makes conscious use may be compared to a stick by the aid of which a blind man gropes his way. And language, taken as a whole, becomes the gateway to a new world. All progress here opens a new perspec-

> tive and widens and enriches our
> concrete experience. Eagerness and
> enthusiasm to talk do not originate in
> a mere desire for learning or using
> names; they mark the desire for the
> detection and conquest of an objective
> world.
>
> ERNST CASSIRER, *An Essay on Man*

Children's perceptions and use of language have the quality of making wildly imaginative leaps; metaphors are created as the child observes and constructs his or her world in language. Ruth Lechlinter catches that in a visual example in this excerpt from her poem "Drawing by Ronnie C., Grade One":

For the sky, blue, but the six-year-old
searching his crayon-box, finds
no blue to match that sky
framed by the window—a see-through shine
over treetops, housetops. The way colors
hold only dead light, not this water-flash
thinning to silver
at morning's far edge.
Gray won't do, either:
gray is for rain that you make with
dark slanting lines down-paper
                    Try orange!

For the six-year-old child, it is easy to imagine the sky orange, to see a zebra in a mongrel, or a castle in a cloud; for an adult, it is much more difficult.

But as a writer, you can preserve, recapture, and heighten that ability. Note the visions in these brief descriptions by the poet Charles Reznikoff:

The house-wreckers have left the door and a staircase,
now leading to the empty room of night

                    •   •   •

Walk about the subway station
in a grove of steel pillars;
how their knobs, the rivet-heads—
unlike those of oaks—
are regularly placed:
how barren the ground is

except here and there on the platform
a flat black fungus
that was chewing gum.

CHARLES REZNIKOFF
By the Waters of Manhattan

One can find fresh visions anywhere—in the subway, when view-
ing a demolished house, when watching a bird. The limiting factor is one's vision, not the sights one sees.

It is essential for a writer unceasingly to study men, and it is a fault
in me that I find it often a very
tedious business. It requires a great
deal of patience. There are of course
men of marked idiosyncrasy who offer
themselves to your observation with
all the precision of a finished picture, they are "characters," striking
and picturesque figures; and they
often take pleasure in displaying
their peculiarity, as though they
amused themselves and wanted you to
share their amusement. But they are
few. They stand out from the common
run and have at once the advantage and
the disadvantage of the exceptional.
What they have in vividness they are
apt to lack in verisimilitude. To
study the average man is an affair of
quite another sort. He is strangely
amorphous. There is someone there,
with a character of his own, standing
on his own feet, with a hundred
peculiarities; but the picture is hazy
and confused. Since he does not know
himself, how can he tell you anything
about himself? However talkative, he
is inarticulate. Whatever treasures
he has to offer you he conceals with
all the more effectiveness that he
does not know they are treasures. If
you want to make a man out of these
crowded shadows, as a sculptor makes
a statue from a block of stone, you
want time, patience, a Chinese ingenu-

ity and a dozen qualities besides.
You must be ready to listen for hours
to the retailing of second-hand information in order at last to catch
the hint or the casual remark that
betrays. Really to know men you must
be interested in them for their own
sake rather than for yours, so that
you care for what they say just
because they say it.

W. SOMERSET MAUGHAM, *A Writer's Notebook*

The writer needs to see people with openness and freshness of vision. Somerset Maugham is, of course, discussing character from a novelist's point of view when he speaks of the ease or difficulty with which real life characters can be shaped for fictional uses. But much of what he says is applicable to other writing as well, and assuredly "it is essential for a writer unceasingly to study men." Interaction with other human beings is essential to human growth and provides a major way for people to test out the validity of their experiences.

How does one "see" character? If you are a mystery reader, you will recall the amazing powers of perception of Sherlock Holmes.

"Come in!" said Holmes.

A man entered who could hardly have been less than six feet six inches in height, with a chest and limbs of Hercules. His dress was rich with a richness which would, in England, be looked upon as akin to bad taste. Heavy bands of astrakhan were slashed across the sleeves and fronts of his double-breasted coat, while the deep blue cloak which was thrown over his shoulders was lined with flame-coloured silk and secured at the neck with a brooch which consisted of a single flaming beryl. Boots which extended halfway up his calves, and which were trimmed at the tops with rich brown fur completed the impression of barbaric opulence which was suggested by his whole appearance. He carried a broadbrimmed hat in his hand, while he wore across the upper part of his face, extending down past the cheek-bones, a black vizard mask, which he had apparently adjusted that very moment for his hand was still raised to it as he entered. From the lower part of the face he appeared to be a man of strong character, with a thick hanging lip, and a long, straight chin suggestive of resolution pushed to the length of obstinacy.

ARTHUR CONAN DOYLE, "A Scandal in Bohemia"

Ah, would that the universe of the writer were populated with such characters, six feet six, barbarically opulent, with cape and jewels, and of course wearing a mask. Would too, that one had the power of reading chins which allowed Holmes to detect (quite accurately as it turns out) that this character was possessed of "resolution pushed to the length of obstinacy."

Obviously, Holmes's powers were created by Arthur Conan Doyle, in part as a literary device to introduce new characters. (Note, for example, that Doyle poses the character at the door, hand raised to the mask, and freezes him there for a paragraph of observation.) Indeed, even with these contrived powers, Holmes's vision was limited to what most of us would label superficialities —details of geography and employment—and Doyle was singularly narrow in his characterizations: Most of the people who crossed the stage were stereotypes—the Rich-but-Foolish, Innocents, Arch-Villains, Master Criminals, Dirty-but-Good-Hearted Urchins, and so on.

The magic of language allows us to catch the world, stop it, and examine it. Language not only frames the picture; it invests meaning as well. If we fight to maintain freshness of vision, avoiding the stereotypical and the confirmed, our language will possess the same kinds of freshness.

DISCUSSION

There are no rules for developing insights and using imaginative language when one encounters the world, but one can recognize such qualities when they appear. Here is a collection of passages from the works of professional writers that seem to us to "have it." Read through these portraits and discuss what you see as the imaginative insights and the creative uses of language in each.

He was one of those who attract by their movement, whose movement is watched unconsciously, as we watch the flight of a seabird waving its wing leisurely.

D. H. LAWRENCE, "The Old Adam"

When I first became aware of Mrs. Albright in my world—at the age of three or four, I suppose—she was almost seventy, and a figure calculated to excite the retina and linger in the consciousness of any child. Aunt Margery, as everybody called her, was stout and round,

and in the phrase of one of her friends, set close to the ground like
a cabbage. Her shortness was curiously exaggerated by the effect
of an early injury. She had fractured her right kneecap in a fall on
the ice when she was in her late teens, and the leg remained twisted,
so that, when she was standing, she bent over as if she were about
to lean down and tie her shoelace, and her torso swayed from side to
side when she walked, like the slow pendulum of an ancient clock,
arousing sympathy in the old and wonder in the young.

JAMES THURBER, "Daguerrotype of a Lady"

I fell in love with London at about 4:00 p.m. on a gray silken day
in the late spring of 1922, and have been in love with it ever
since. . . .

This stupendous capital is, to my mind, the greatest city in the
world. It isn't as old as Rome, as luminous as Paris, as spectacular
as New York, or as big as Tokyo. It has all manner of negative
qualities, like the weather (ever seen a true West End Londoner
without an umbrella?), its provincialism (like the licensing hours in
pubs), and its archaic preoccupation with classes; nobody can be
more of a snob than a true Cockney. Nevertheless, it has grace,
durability, style and above all, formidable weight. It knows what true
satisfactions are.

JOHN GUNTHER, *Inside London*

I am in love with Montana. For other states I have admiration,
respect, recognition, even some affection, but with Montana it
is love, and it's difficult to analyze love when you're in it. Once
when I raptured in a violet glow given off by the Queen of the World,
my father asked me why, and I thought he was crazy not to see.
Of course I know now she was a mouse-haired, freckle-nosed,
scabby-kneed little girl with a voice like a bat and the loving kindness
of a gila monster, but then she lighted up the landscape and me.
It seems to me that Montana is a great splash of grandeur. It is huge
but not overpowering. The land is rich with grass and color, and
the mountains are the kind I would create if mountains were ever
put on my agenda. Montana seems to me to be what a small boy
would think Texas is like from hearing Texans.

JOHN STEINBECK, *Travels with Charley*

Karen had stared around at her sister. Celine was twenty-six now,
but looked older. She had always seemed older to Karen, who was
nine years younger, but this morning her thin little eyebrows, her
moist eyes, her flat cheeks, seemed those of a woman who had never
known youth. I will never look like that, Karen thought clearly.

JOYCE CAROL OATES, *With Shuddering Fall*

A Teacher's got a temper
like a bull.
He growls and roars
like a tiger,
he stamps and gets mad
and sometimes he's glad
he did it.
> BRUCE MACGREGOR, age 9, from *Miracles*

A library table I particularly admire is at Scandinavian Design,
15 East 53rd Street. It is a pure, light lovely table, designed by Bruno
Mathsson, with a birch frame and legs and a top made of ash—
a smooth, straight-grained almost white wood that resembles
unfinished white pine but narrowly escapes pine's look of rawness.
The difference is a subtle one; perhaps it can be said that the ash
looks nude, while pine looks naked. The top (seventy-one inches long
and thirty inches wide) has gently rounded edges, and the legs
widen slightly as they ascend, and do something interesting just
before they reach the top; they suddenly split in two and the halves
bend back like opening flower petals to receive the tabletop upon
their uplifted surfaces. The price is $397, and the table can be ordered
in other shapes and sizes at other prices. It is finished with invisible
coats of lacquer and plastic shellac, and the wood is supposed not to
darken very much. In the showroom, it stands near a window, and
this seems appropriate, for everything about the table is reflective
of daylight and air and space.
> J. M., "About The House," *The New Yorker*

WRITING IDEAS AND EXPERIMENTS

Assume that you are, in Whitman's sense, a child "going forth"
   into the world. Make a catalogue of all the things you encounter on a long walk and show how they do or do not "become
   a part" of you.

Probably at some time each day, you pause because your attention has suddenly been caught by the way the sunlight reflects
   in a pool of rainwater, or by the sound a tire makes as a car
   turns, or by the way a half-torn letter is blown by the wind down
   a dirty street. Try to distill such a moment into a line or two.
   (Be sure that you begin with one of your own moments and
   not with a secondhand one like those above.)

Select an object—your desk, a tree, a lamp post, a statue, a stair-
   way, the entrance to a building—and concentrate your attention on it until you feel that you have isolated it and imaginatively penetrated and outlined it. Then describe it either in a

paragraph of prose or in a poem, capturing as much as you can of the essence of the object.

Place yourself at "center stage"—a busy corridor, a restaurant, a sporting event—and watch the drama. Jot down notes on the cast of characters that comes by. At a later time, you might want to take this dramatis personae and develop a play or short story around them.

Write a drama in which you are the central character, and you are seated in the center of a bare stage talking with various fictional characters who come by. Use this setting to write about yourself, to demonstrate your "self" as it interacts (or as you would like it to interact) with people.

Choose a person, and with (or without) the person's knowledge, study him or her closely enough to write a detailed portrait, or character sketch.

Write a portrait or profile of someone especially close to you. Include enough detail so that an outsider can sense your relationship to the person.

FURTHER POINTS OF DEPARTURE

In your reading of fiction, look for interesting, vivid, or unusual descriptions of people, places, and things. Collect them to create your own writer's gallery. Describe some of the techniques—perceptual and literary—that writers use to convey their encounters with the world.

Do the same for autobiography or nonfiction. Do writers of fiction and nonfiction differ in the ways they see and report their worlds?

In Japan, almost everyone writes haiku, not because people consider themselves poets, but because the writing of these poems serves a personal need. To cultivate your sense of vision, try writing haiku. You might become a haiku addict; there are worse fates for an aspiring writer.
Bashō wrote:

Spring too, very soon!
   They are setting the scene for it—
      Plum tree and moon.

Write a haiku announcing the coming of winter, autumn, or summer.

Here are two other Bashō haiku:

> A sudden lightning gleam:
>> off into the darkness goes
>>> the night heron's scream.

· · ·

> Song of the cuckoo:
>> in the grove of great bamboos,
>>> moonlight seeping through.

Explore the different effects of these two haiku and show why they differ. Write a pair of contrasting haiku, and then explain how you deliberately created differing effects.

Here is another of Charles Reznikoff's visions:

> About an excavation
> a flock of bright red lanterns
> has settled.

One can also become addicted to collecting short images of this sort. Set aside some pages in a writing notebook and jot down similar kinds of observations from your own experience. One writer who noted such items was F. Scott Fitzgerald. You might enjoy reading from his writing notebooks, published in *The Crack Up* (New Directions).

Interweaving
the world

Perhaps the quickest way to understand
the elements of what a novelist is
doing is not to read, but to write;
to make your own experiment with the
dangers and difficulties of words.
Recall, then, some event that has left
a distinct impression on you—how at
the corner of the street, perhaps,
you passed two people talking. A tree
shook; an electric light danced; the
tone of the talk was comic, but also
tragic; a whole vision, an entire
conception, seemed contained in that
moment.

But when you attempt to reconstruct it
in words, you will find that it breaks
into a thousand conflicting impressions. Some must be subdued; others
emphasized; in the process you will
lose, probably, all grasp upon the
emotion itself.

VIRGINIA WOOLF, *The Second Common Reader*

We not only encounter the world but become involved and
entangled with the people, events, and objects that make up one
world. We find ourselves in an endless web of relationships and
associations. As individuals grow, they spend their lives interweaving—largely through language—the elements of their worlds
to create complete pictures.

We spin out circles in our daily human involvements, which

develop, establish, and bring to fruition involvements that go beyond our actual physical presence.

> All life . . . comes back to the
> question of our speech, the medium
> through which we communicate with each
> other; for all life comes back to the
> question of our relations with each
> other. These relations are made pos-
> sible, are registered, are verily
> constituted, by our speech, and are
> successful . . . in proportion as our
> speech is worthy of its great human
> and social function; is developed,
> delicate, flexible, rich—an adequate
> accomplished fact. The more it sug-
> gests and expresses the more we live
> by it—the more it promotes and
> enhances life. Its quality, its
> authenticity, its security, are hence
> supremely important for the general
> multifold opportunity, for the dignity
> and integrity, of our existence.
>
> HENRY JAMES, "The Question of Our Speech"

We begin at home with the family; and starting from this
center, create ever-widening circles of social involvement. In the
neighborhood we have casual and informal associations with
those nearby—people with whom we discuss politics, taxes, street-
cleaning, armchair philosophy, from whom we borrow a typewriter and to whom we lend our newest album. There are also
"neighborhoods" that the individual enters wherever he or she
spends time—at a job, in school, at a library; these circles of
friends and acquaintances form other linguistic and social webs.
Beyond the neighborhoods of the individual is the town or city;
beyond the city, the county; and beyond the county, the state,
country, world, universe. Although all of us come to view ourselves as living within some such hierarchy of structures as this,
we seldom stop to realize that these structures are mental and are
given order and pattern primarily by language. Who has ever
seen the state, or the world, whole? We know they exist because
we hold the words that name them in our heads.

As people grow from childhood to adulthood, their range of
vision increases because of their broadened experiences and be-

cause maturity brings increased powers of abstraction, which allow one to grasp and understand ideas beyond the immediate vision. As philosopher-psychologist Jean Piaget has observed, people go through stages of mental growth as they move from childhood's self-centered world of objects and actions to the world of the adult, who is capable of abstracting, valuing, hypothesizing, and relating. As we gain in the ability to abstract, we weave and interweave our world—in essence creating the universe in which we live.

Interweaving the world is art, not science; there are no firm rules for the process, and thus perceptions, abstractions, and visions differ from one person to another.

MRS. SMITH   Yogurt is excellent for the stomach, the kidneys, the appendicitis, and apotheosis. It was Doctor Mackenzie-King who told me that, he's the one who takes care of the children of our neighbors, the Johns. He's a good doctor. One can trust him. He never prescribes any medicine that he's not tried out on himself first. Before operating on Parker, he had his own liver operated on first, although he was not the least bit ill.

MR. SMITH   But how does it happen that the doctor pulled through while Parker died?

MRS. SMITH   Because the operation was successful in the doctor's case and it was not in Parker's.

MR. SMITH   Then Mackenzie is not a good doctor. The operation should have succeeded with both of them or else both should have died.

MRS. SMITH   Why?

MR. SMITH   A conscientious doctor must die with his patient if they can't get well together. The captain of a ship goes down with his ship into the briny deep, he does not survive alone.

MRS. SMITH   One cannot compare a patient with a ship.

MR. SMITH   Why not? A ship has its diseases too; moreover, your doctor is as hale as a ship; that's why he should have perished at the same time as his patient, like the captain and his ship.

MRS. SMITH   Ah! I hadn't thought of that. . . . Perhaps it is true. . . . Ah then, what conclusion do you draw from this?

MR. SMITH   All doctors are quacks. And all patients, too. Only the Royal Navy is honest in England.

EUGÈNE IONESCO, *The Bald Soprano*

In this excerpt from Eugene Ionesco's antiplay *The Bald Soprano,* we see two people who have woven worlds quite different

from the ones most of us inhabit. Although Mr. Smith may have
a point in suggesting that all doctors (and patients) are quacks,
the perceptions and abstractions he employs in reaching that conclusion are so far removed from reality that we probably think
(as Ionesco wants us to) that the argument is nonsensical.

Where, when, and how does one separate sense from nonsense, reality from unreality, sanity from insanity? We live much
of our adult lives in a web of thought and perception that is outside the real world; our principal access to this web is language.
We constantly inhabit the space and time both around and beyond us through imaginative projections via language. We all are
visionaries, historians, prophets in some degree, even though our
frame of reference is limited to ourselves. We know about or speculate on what lies beyond our personal sight; we have a conception of that past which casts us as the central figure and hero;
and we have some conception of the future that will feel our
presence.

> Human civilization is an outgrowth of
> language, and language is the product
> of advancing civilization. Freedom
> of thought is made possible by lan-
> guage; we are thereby released from
> complete bondage to the immediacies
> of mood and circumstance.
>
> ALFRED NORTH WHITEHEAD, *Modes of Thought*

There is much to be said for becoming conscious where we
are unconscious, for becoming aware where we are unaware. In
other words, the patterns which we have spun out for ourselves
might remain a muddle in our minds, or they might be spread out
on a page and be examined. The very process of putting them on a
page will reveal contradictions and impossibilities that will force
clarity. As Eldridge Cleaver remarked, "[I write] to seek out the
truth and unravel the snarled web of my motivation."

We are all involved in interweaving our worlds in language.
Indeed, the nature of our lives will be determined in large part by
the way we interweave and create our worlds, and the consciousness with which we do it.

DISCUSSION

The epigraph by Henry James begins: "All life . . . comes back to
the question of our speech." This is an extravagant claim. Ex-

plain insofar as you can what James means, and use your own "life" to examine the applicability of his point.

Discuss the hierarchy of people and structures that constitute your world. Who are the people closest to you? the institutions and events? How do you weave them into your own view of the world? How is your view of the world shaped and redirected by them?

What is reality? Who creates it? Who determines it? Who arbitrates different views of reality?

Speculate on the role of language in creating a reality that lives beyond your actual range of vision. You have, perhaps, a conception of Washington, D.C., without ever having been there. It is an entity with a shape in your imagination. How did it get there? How much did language contribute to the shape of the image?

WRITING IDEAS AND EXPERIMENTS

Create a drama or short story involving characters whose perceptions of the world differ so greatly that they cannot communicate with each other. Such a scene may have comic overtones, but it can just as easily produce tragedy.

Write a scene from an antiplay which defies the logic of the universe.

Recall a setting that was initially frightening or sinister, but which became routine and boring after repeated encounters. Capture, if you can, the original feelings and the details of the setting that inspired them. Then show the reality that changed the apprehension into boredom.

How much do you live your life in the future? Write a scenario—a fantasy, a satire, a prediction—for your future. Finish with a critique of the scenario, which includes some estimation of the chances of its actually being played out.

Design a utopia, an ideal world, to match your vision of how the world should be woven.

FURTHER POINTS OF DEPARTURE

Reread the epigraph by Virginia Woolf and try the experiment she suggests reconstructing a past event, or moment, which was important to you. After you have called up the details and captured the moment, evaluate the experience in relation to the predictions in her second paragraph—that, for example, in the process of putting thoughts in language you will probably lose "all grasp upon the emotion" felt in the actual event.

In one of the notable modern American novels, Ralph Ellison's *Invisible Man,* the hero (who remains nameless throughout) lives through a series of nightmare experiences in which other individuals attempt to use them and to thrust a ready-made identity on him. He resists, survives, endures, and, moreover, comes finally to a sense of self-awareness and self-identity.

> And now all past humiliations became precious parts of my experience, and for the first time, leaning against that stone wall in the sweltering night, I began to accept my past and, as I accepted it, I felt memories welling up within me. It was as though I'd learned suddenly to look around corners; images of past humiliations flickered through my head and I saw that they were more than separate experiences. They were me; they defined me, and no blind men, no matter how powerful they became, even if they conquered the world, could take that, or change one single itch, taunt, laugh, cry, scar, ache, range or pain of it.

Are you able to look at your own life in the way that Ellison's Invisible Man is here looking at his?
  a. Write an account of your identity in the terms he uses to define himself—your experiences, or your encounters with the world, and the scars they left.
  b. Compare the idea of identity contained in this passage from Ellison's *Invisible Man* with that contained in Whitman's "There Was a Child Went Forth."

Read Ellison's *Invisible Man* and explore the ways in which his experiences gave him the identity he discovers at the end of the book—an identity different from any offered him or forced on him by individuals trying to use him.

Film allows unique experiences in seeing and abstracting from reality. Using movie or still cameras (one or several), photograph a scene or event from multiple vantage points—close, distant, low, high. How does visual viewpoint affect both one's perception of reality and abstraction from it?

Exploring/
probing/
researching

Is it possible to . . . forsee the
learning society? This would be one
that, in addition to offering part-
time adult education to every man and
woman at every stage of grownup life,
had succeeded in transforming its
value in such a way that learning,
fulfillment, becoming human, had become
its aims and all its institutions
were directed to this end. This is
what the Athenians did. They did not
content themselves with the limited,
peripheral effort of providing part-
time education to everybody at every
stage of life. They made their society
one designed to bring all its members
to the fullest development of their
highest powers. By our standards and
in our terms, the Athenians were an
uneducated people; the vast, elaborate,
expensive, highly organized instruc-
tional programs and plants of modern
times were unknown to them. They did
not have much of an educational system. But they have been the educators
of the human race. In Athens, education was not a segregated activity,
conducted for certain hours, in certain
places, at a certain time of life.
It was the aim of the society. The
city educated the man. The Athenian
was educated by the culture, by
<u>paideia.</u>

ROBERT MAYNARD HUTCHINS, *The Learning Society*

> Why do I feel so irritated by this
> University? They keep on telling us
> that the post-graduate year will give
> us a chance to "reexamine our basic
> assumptions" . . . which is pretty
> patronizing. How do they know I don't
> spend all my time agonizing over my
> basic assumptions? Why after all did
> I come here?
>
> Well why?
>
> It was not quite the normal course of
> events, I suppose. At Cambridge the
> people I knew who decided to stay on
> and do post-graduate certificate gave
> various reasons which were nothing to
> do with education: another year of
> Cambridge cricket, or a girl friend
> who still had a year to do at Homerton.
>
> NICHOLAS OTTY, *Learner Teacher*

The *learning society* is a concept that has had appeal to cultures throughout recorded history. It is, as Robert Maynard Hutchins describes it, a society where learning is continuous throughout one's lifetime, where a culture becomes sufficiently attuned to the needs of the individual that it concentrates its energies on "learning, fulfillment, [and] becoming human." John Gardner has spoken of a "self-renewing" society in which all citizens are engaged in a constant process of intellectual rejuvenation, where attitudes and values are such that individuals (and thus the society as a whole) are constantly engaged in a process of assessing their current growth and development and seeking out new experiences. The learning society is one that continues to grow, not in terms of gross national product or bigger and better automobile engines, but spiritually, emotionally, and intellectually.

"Is it possible to . . . forsee the learning society?" Hutchins asks, and most of us would agree that our society presently exhibits few of the traits of a self-renewing society. Gardner describes what happens to many people:

"Keep on growing," the commencement speakers say.
"Don't go to seed. Let this be a beginning, not an ending."

It is a good theme. Yet a high proportion of the young people who hear the speeches pay no heed, and by the time they are middle aged, they are absolutely mummified. Some of the people who are making the speeches are mummified.

JOHN GARDNER, *Self-Renewal*

For an alarmingly large percentage of the population, high school graduation is the high point of life, the apex of accomplishment, and an end to individual growth, after which they settle into lives of "quiet desperation." Other people remain self-renewing through college, through their twenties, thirties or forties, but eventually become mummified, settling into a stale existence where exploring/probing/researching comes to a halt.

Why does this happen? When we look at young children, we can see clearly that all normal members of humanity are born curious, with an innate desire to learn and explore. What happens to people to destroy this "intellectual curiosity"?

It has been attributed to an experience common to most North Americans: entering the educational system for ten or twelve or sixteen or twenty years. The experiences alluded to by Otty at the beginning of this chapter are not rare, and as numerous critics of education have pointed out, the schools frequently produce end products—people—with characteristics precisely opposite those aimed for by the school system. The schools intend to produce literate, inquiring minds, and they create illiterate persons who are closed to new experiences.

School, after all, is the one institution in our society that is inflicted on everybody, and what happens in school makes a difference—for good or ill. We use the word "inflicted" because we believe that the way schools are currently conducted does very little, and probably nothing, to enhance our chances of mutual survival. . . . The institution we call "school" is what it is because we made it that way. If it is irrelevant, as Marshall McLuhan says; if it shields children from reality, as Norbert Wiener says; if it educates for obsolescence, as John Gardner says; if it does not develop intelligence, as John

> Holt says; if it avoids the promotion
> of significant learnings, as Carl
> Rogers says; if it induces alienation,
> as Paul Goodman says; if it punishes
> creativity and independence, as Edgar
> Friedenberg says; if, in short, it is
> not doing what needs to be done, it
> can be changed; it <u>must</u> be changed.
>
> NEAL POSTMAN and CHARLES WEINGARTNER,
> *Teaching as a Subversive Activity*

But it would be a gross oversimplification to blame the school system, for it is clear that the schools reflect the attitudes and values of society, particularly the values that society places on knowledge. We chose verbs for this chapter title—"Explor*ing*, Prob*ing*, Research*ing*"—for we are convinced that one reason Western culture has not been successful in achieving a learning society is that it has habitually placed emphasis on *knowledge*—a noun, a thing—rather than on *knowing*—a process. Since the industrial revolution of the eighteenth and nineteenth centuries, we have been deeply obsessed with the accumulation of vast bodies of knowledge, particularly knowledge which has a practical, or applied, orientation. This has led to enormous technological achievements, most notably the flying of three human beings 285,000 miles into outer space for purposes of landing on an inert planetoid.

> Clearly, science represents a type of
> knowledge with absolute priority over
> all others, and I myself take great
> pains to work scientifically. But at
> the same time I can't help thinking
> that science would be more appealing
> if it had no practical use. In what
> we call progress, 90 per cent of our
> efforts go into finding a cure for the
> harms linked to the advantages brought
> about by the remaining 10 per cent.
>
> CLAUDE LÉVI-STRAUSS

Yet this concern for product and for progress has also had unfortunate—almost disastrous—side effects in creating a planet that is increasingly unlivable for its underfed and far-too-numerous inhabitants.

> Almost every important invention unbalances the font of progress, and a new invention is needed to redress the balance. . . .
>   **DENNIS GABOR**

How does knowing/researching/probing take place successfully? *Can* we know how it takes place successfully? Why was Louis Pasteur able to conceptualize "molecules" simply by seeing tartaric acid crystals that were mirror images of each other under his microscope? Why did Charles Goodyear, cleaning up a hot stove on which he had spilled some latex, recognize a new property of stretchiness that led him to discover the vulcanization of rubber? What processes of knowing led Shakespeare to write *Hamlet,* Beethoven to compose his Ninth Symphony, or Hieronymus Bosch to paint the *Triptych*?

Obviously every "subject," every field of knowledge, has its own basic patterns of knowing—of perceiving experience—and one of the aims of education (a good education, at any rate) is to help the student become competent in the basic patterns of knowing. Pasteur, for example, was following a well-established set of procedures—the scientific method—when he made his discoveries. So, too, there is basic knowledge unique to each field that one uses in exploring new dimensions of that field. Shakespeare drew on the Hollingshead Chronicles and the conventions of the Elizabethan theatre; and Beethoven obviously knew harmonic structures and the traditions of symphonic composing.

> If your experience isn't strange to you, it's false.
>   **ANDRÉ BRETON**

What cannot be identified easily, however, is the spark that leads beyond background knowledge and mastery of basic processes. To use the term we have employed throughout this book, one must have the *imagination* to see things from a fresh point of view, to treat all experience, as Breton suggests, as if it is "strange." We do know that when one gives the imagination free reign and does not become bound by set conventions of knowledge, ideas emerge, not always brilliant or even unique and seldom on schedule, but based on the individual's own perceptions and understandings. When that happens, exploring/probing/researching is successful, and equally important, the language that one uses to write about his or her perceptions in reality comes alive.

DISCUSSION

C. P. Snow has written of "the two cultures," science and the humanities, and the traditional rivalry and incompatibility between them. Alan McGlashan says of the relationship:

> The marriage between thinking and feeling can take place only at the deepest level of the psyche. In everyday life, these two functions tend to be antagonistic except in certain moments of high crisis. And while this is so, human consciousness is a crippled thing. Moreover, when operating in isolation, each function is essentially destructive. The thermonuclear bomb is a typical endproduct of the kind of thinking that is disconnected from feeling.

Need there be a separation between the two cultures?

Discuss your own patterns for exploring/probing/researching. How do you go about seeking answers to problems that you face? What techniques and strategies do you use to expand your own horizons?

Do we want a learning society? What would happen to life as we know it if all members of society were self-renewing in ways we have described here?

Compare your school learning experiences with those outside the classroom. How do your learning patterns differ in school and life? Are there discrepancies?

Bring in for discussion notes, drafts, or final copy of papers you are being asked to write in other classes. Examine the writing style you use in other courses and compare it to the one you employ when doing experiments for *Writing in Reality*. Consider ways you can make connections between the best of your personal writing and the writing you do for academic courses.

WRITING IDEAS AND EXPERIMENTS

Write a utopian vision of "the learning society." What would it be like? (Consider doing this experiment as science fiction.)

Write an essay tracing your experiences in the schools and show how this has influenced your ways of learning and knowing.

Every generation of writers produces scores of essays on how to rear children (and, of course, every generation feels it can do a better job of it than the previous one). Now it's your turn: Write an essay giving your views on how to raise children.

Choose a topic about which you already know a considerable amount. It could range from baton twirling or downhill skiing to the history of water power or the Brazilian political system. Write a series of exploratory questions for a person new to the field; group them under the headings used in this book:

a. Discussion
b. Writing (or other) Ideas and Experiments
c. Further Points of Departure

Can you "teach" other people to explore/probe/research and learn through such questions?

FURTHER POINTS OF DEPARTURE

In exploring/probing/researching, knowing how and where to find information is frequently as important as the actual writing. In order to strengthen your own skills at finding materials, choose an unfamiliar topic from the list below and search the library card catalog for resources. What is available? Prepare a brief, one page bibliography on the topic (or, read some of the materials and write a one page introductory article in the manner of an encyclopedia entry):

Abberdeen-Angus	Cacti
Addiction	Child abuse
Agnosticism	Church of England
Arctic expeditions	Corfam
Ballads	Cybernetics
Baton twirling	Demography
Berlin Wall	Demonology
Blake, William	Demosthenes
Brazilian politics	Earth shine
Brewing	Editing

Electronic data processing
Erosion
Experimental stress analysis
Feminism
Fencing
Food synthesis
Formic acid
Genetic cloning
Geology of your state
Gordon, Flash
Grammar
Griffith, D. W.
Hamburgers
Haydn, Joseph
Holograms
Home construction
Intelligence quotient
Investment portfolio
Irish Republican Army
James, Henry
James, Jesse
James, William
Japanese cooking
Knighthood
Knight's Penny Magazine
Linotype
Long, Huey
Lymphatics
Lysergic Acid Diethylamide
Malpractice
Marathon
Mice
Microphotography
Needles
Noodles
Nothingness
Occupational therapy
Oratorio
Origami
Overtime
Pain
Paint
Personality test
Program budgeting

Quakers
Queuing theory
Quartets, barber shop
Quartets, string
Reconstruction
Regeneration
Robin redbreast
Rope making
Sand
Salt
School furniture
Search and seizure
Table manners
Timber harvest
Tumbling
Tungsten
United Nations
Universal joint
Universal suffrage
Urban renewal
Vandalism
Violin construction
Virginity
Voyage of H.M.S. Beagle
Walking
Water power
Water skiing
Weather forecasting
Williams, Esther
Williams, Ted
Williams, William Carlos
Wheel, the
X-Rays
Xerox
Xerxes
Xylotomy
Yarn
Yeats, William Butler
Yucatan
Zebra
Zero
Zionism
Zoology

Causes and commitments

While the traffic jams of rush hour
continued to clog the cities'
streets, and their exhausts to foul
the air, the four winds still
follow the way of the Great Spirit,
And while bulldozers continued to rape
our Mother Earth and loggers to
cut our forests, Nature still
follows the way of the Great Spirit,
And while dams were being erected
across the rivers blocking the
return of the spawning fish, the
fish still fight to follow the
instructions and ways of the Great
Spirit,
And while factories and industries
were doing their share to pollute
our waters, our air, and our land,
thus destroying the works of the
Great Spirit,
And while people continued their in-
sane dreams for power and riches
at the cost of others, of their own
brothers, which is not the way of
the Great Spirit,
And while the sun was blistering the
leaves of trees and turning the
grasses yellow across the Great
Plains, and shrinking the waters of
many lakes and rivers across this
turtle island continent of the
Great Spirit;

In the month of July, while people
    turned to the waters to cool them-
    selves of the summer heat;
Apache, Cheyenne, Hopi, Sioux, Mayan;
Puyallup, and Nisqually,
    Together, as the eagle and the sky,
Tulalip, Eskimo, Umatilla, Pomo,
Klamath, Coeur d'Alene, and Quinault,
    children of the Great Spirit, we
    did gather, as the four winds,
Walla Walla, Shoshone, Blackfoot,
Paiute, Potawatomi, Mohawk, and
Lumbee,
    together we gathered, as brothers
    and sisters, as the allness of
    nature,
Pitt River, Suswap, Cherokee Nation,
Muckleshoot, Snoqualmie, Yakima, and
Tuscarora,
    together to form the circle, the
    hoop, the sacred roundness of all
    Indian peoples.
Sac and Fox, Omaha, Mescalero, Pima,
Onondaga, Iowa, Nootka, Salish,
Quechan, Pueblo, Hoopa, Wintun, Algon-
quin, Seneca, and Cree,
    we came to listen and to speak,
Shusap, Lummi, Tlinget, Penobscot,
Comanche, Montagnais, and Stilligu-
amish,
    there, in the far away land of the
    northwest, on the shores of the big
    waters, we met as guests of the
    Tulalip people. In the longhouse
    of the Tulalip, we sat to council;
Kiowa, Warm Springs, Canada Blackfoot
and Cree, Samish, Chippewa, Duwamish,
and Shawnee.
To council and to listen to the elders
    of our many tribes,
To hear the prophecies of our tradi-
    tional people and to share our many
    common ties,
We the people of the land, the true
    children of our Earth Mother,
    because we are the very land.
We met to learn and to bring to light
    the many problems facing our people.

As our Mother Earth is being destroyed
and contaminated, and as the Great
Spirit grows angry at this waste
and greed,
We met, not to weep over today and
yesterday, but to plan and to
create a better future for our
children,
We met, as guardians of this turtle
island continent to renew our
strength and courage in the face of
all that is evil in this day and
age.

Statement of the North American Indian
Unity Conference, Summer 1970

Fellow Citizens, we are asking you to
join with us in our attempt to better
the lives of all Indian people.

We are on Alcatraz Island to make
known to the world that we have a
right to use our land for our own
benefit.

In a proclamation of November 20, 1969,
we told the government of the United
States that we are here "to create a
meaningful use for our Great Spirit's
land."

We, the native Americans, reclaim the
land known as Alcatraz Island in the
name of all American Indians by the
right of discovery.

We wish to be fair and honorable in
our dealings with the Caucasian inhabitants of this land, and hereby
offer the following treaty:

We will purchase said Alcatraz Island
for twenty-four dollars ($24) in glass
beads and red cloth, a precedent set
by the white man's purchase of a
similar island about 300 years ago.
We know that $24 in trade goods for
these 16 acres is more than was paid
when Manhattan Island was sold, but we

know that land values have risen over
the years.   Our offer of $1.24 per
acre is greater than the 47¢ per acre
the white men are now paying the
California Indians for their land. . . .

Some of the present buildings will be
taken over to develop an American
Indian museum which will depict our
native food and other cultural contributions we have given to the world.
Another part of the museum will present
some of the things the white man has
done to the Indian in return for the
land and life he took: disease, alco-
hol, poverty, and cultural decimation
(as symbolized by old tin cans, barbed
wire, rubber tires, plastic containers,
etc.).   Part of the museum will remain
a dungeon to symbolize those Indian
captives who were incarcerated for
challenging white authority and those
who were imprisoned on reservations.
The museum will show the noble and
tragic events of Indian history, including the broken treaties, the
documentary of the Trail of Tears, the
Massacre of Wounded Knee, as well as
the victory over Yellow-Hair Custer
and his army.

In the name of all Indians, therefore,
we reclaim this island for our Indian
nations, for all these reasons.   We
feel the claim is just and proper, and
that this land should rightfully be
granted to us for as long as the
rivers run and the sun shall shine.

We hold the Rock!

> Statement issued by Indians of all Nations
> following the claiming of Alcatraz Island under
> federal "discovery" laws, Fall 1969

Since a person's view of the world is created by the meshing
of his or her own thoughts, observations, and perceptions, the
inevitable result is that different worlds are created by different
people. Because of differences in experience, cultural setting, up-
bringing, and the like, people's value systems differ dramatically.

We develop sets of beliefs and become involved in causes and commitments as they harmonize or conflict with our values. We come together in groups and associations to promote a cause or to fight for, or against, one: We sit down and talk, we stand up and argue, we harangue a crowd, and we hurl epithets at each other in defense of our cause. Some people proclaim a cause not for the cause itself but for the value of associating with those in the service of the cause. Others are so obsessed with a cause that they cannot subordinate themselves to any group in which there might be some slight heresy. There are rigid believers so obsessed with their version of the world that they can tolerate no questioning of their truth; they are willing to use any and every means to achieve the universal establishment of their version as official and enforced dogma. There are more flexible people who are willing to entertain challenge, to examine the ideas created by other minds, to admit self-doubt as well as general doubt, to change when convinced that they are wrong in part or in whole. There are weak believers who, having no convictions and little basis for forming them, are willing to shift allegiances, not on the basis of personal loyalties, but on whimsical likes and dislikes.

Frequently in passing from youth to age, people begin as casual believers—essentially flexible—but settle into rigidity of belief. Few people would argue with the assertion that open-minded discussion is better than closed-minded or soft-minded, that flexibility is superior to rigidity. Exchange of views through discussion, encounter, and confrontation are the means for sharpening, refining, and changing beliefs. Since the time in prehistory when man acquired language, it has been generally conceded that these means are superior to the club or the axe. Today, the consensus is that bombast is preferable to bombing and debate better than demolition. Despite the consensus, violence continues to be part of everyday life—in peaceful towns, peacetime cities, and war-torn lands.

Causes and commitments are, ultimately, ways of structuring and giving meaning to our lives; they provide motivation for our actions and explanations for our *re*-actions. Without consciousness of our values and an understanding of their rational and emotional roots, we go through life blindly, attaching ourselves to wrong causes or pursuing commitments without direction.

Marshall McLuhan has noted that as a result of electronic media, we now live in a "global village," a world where we know what our "neighbors" are doing, minute by minute, day by day. Our understanding of causes and commitments becomes even more important, for what happens on the other side of the global village has immediate effects on us and our beliefs and values. Electronic exposure makes us aware of, and draws us into, causes and commitments which previous generations would have ignored. By extending our vision and experience beyond the range known to previous generations, television has led to our increased involvement. The past twenty years has seen an enormous growth in what might be called a public conscience: a willingness to become involved in issues vital to the survival of our global village. Such public concern represents increased individual consciousness.

Wilhelm Stekel: "The mark of the immature man is that he wants to die nobly for a cause, while the mark of the mature man is that he wants to live humbly for one."

Quoted by J. D. SALINGER, *Catcher in the Rye*

If we must die—let it not be like hogs
Hunted and penned in an inglorious
    spot,
While round us bark the mad and hungry
    dogs,
Making their mock at our accursed lot.
If we must die—oh, let us nobly die
So that our precious blood may not be
    shed
In vain; then even the monsters we defy
Shall be constrained to honor us though
    dead!
Oh Kinsmen! We must meet the common
    foe;
Though far outnumbered, let us show
    as brave
And for their thousand blows deal one
    deathblow.
What though before us lies the open
    grave?
Like men we'll face the murderous,
    cowardly pack,
Pressed to the wall, dying, but
    fighting back!

CLAUDE MC KAY, "If We Must Die"

Just as visions of the world differ greatly and lead to commitment to different causes, the ways in which people promote their
causes differ. In your own lifetime you have seen, heard, or experienced dozens, if not hundreds, of ways of promoting a cause:
violent and nonviolent protest, petitions and picketings, zaps and
bombing, armed conflict and orderly debate, strikes, abductions,
teach-ins, sit-ins, terrorism, passive resistance, declamation, as-
sassination, and lawsuits, to name just a few. Having a cause,
one must ask, "How do I promote it?" Do I write a position statement (as did the American Indians at the North American Indian
Unity Conference), or do I take dramatic extralegal action (as
did the American Indians who seized Alcatraz Island to demonstrate their cause)? Is it better, as Wilhelm Stekel believes, to
live humbly for a cause than to die fighting when pushed to the
wall, as Claude McKay argues? Are there limits to rational debate
after which one is justified in turning to violence?

Such questions desperately need resolution, yet conventional
resolutions have seldom proved satisfactory; civilization is—if
one chooses to examine it pessimistically—little more than a record of violent, irrational clashes between value systems, frequently over questions or issues that hardly merit discussion.
While we cannot expect that such clashes can be ended altogether, clearly there is a great need to increase interpersonal communication, for whatever our causes and commitments, we can
be certain that they will all be framed in language.

DISCUSSION

Using the McKay and Stekel quotations, explore the differences
    between the mature and immature person. Are causes things
    to die for?
Debate: Is violence ever justified in support of a cause or com-
    mitment?
Make a catalogue of your basic beliefs and values—a credo, if
    you will. What are the values most central to your life, the
    ones that shape your causes and commitments? Do some ret-
    rospective thinking: Where did these values originate?
Examine your own personality and decide how you would classify
    the strength of your convictions. Have you ever pretended to
    have strong convictions when you did not? Have you ever

feigned disinterest out of anxiety or fear? Are your experiences common to the group?

WRITING IDEAS AND EXPERIMENTS

Choose a single value or a single cause about which you feel strongly. Write a detailed narrative tracing this value through your life, going back as far as you can.

Write a character study of a person you know who is a rigid believer, a flexible believer, or a weak nonbeliever.

Pick an issue or problem in which you believe strongly and write an editorial in support of it.

Wage a debate with yourself on an issue on which you have not made up your mind.

Write a commercial advertisement for a cause that is very important to you.

Send a letter to the editor of a local or campus newspaper.

FURTHER POINTS OF DEPARTURE

It has been persuasively argued that television has become the single, dominant force in shaping the values of our society. Do you agree? Write an essay on the ways in which TV does or doesn't influence values.

Look through the news section of this week's newspaper and make a list of the causes and commitments that are making headlines. What values are represented? Who is promoting what? Why? Do current causes represent self-interest, the interests of humanity, both, or neither?

Explore the role of the family unit in shaping contemporary values. Try demonstrating your ideas by writing a short story or dramatic sketch.

Within two decades, 1940–1960, events occurred that have irrevocably altered man's relationships to other men and to the natural world. The invention of the computer, the successful splitting of the atom and the invention of fission and fusion bombs, the discovery of the biochemistry of the living cell, the exploration of the planet's surface, the extreme acceleration of

population growth and the recognition of the certainty of
catastrophe if it continues, the breakdown in the organization of
cities, the destruction of the natural environment, the linking
up of all parts of the world by means of jet flights and television, the preparations for the building of satellites and the
first steps into space, the newly realized possibilities of unlimited
energy and synthetic raw materials and, in the more advanced
countries, the transformation of man's age-old problems of
production into problems of distribution and consumption—all
these have brought about a drastic, irreversible division between
the generations.

. . . the freeing of men's imagination from the past depends . . .
on the development of a new kind of communication with those
who are most deeply involved with the future—the young who
were born in the new world.

MARGARET MEAD, *Culture and Commitment:*
A Study of the Generation Gap

Assume, as Margaret Mead does, that the older generation has
an imagination fixed on the past, while the younger generation has an imagination fixed on the future. Write an essay
which describes your view of the "new kind of communication" that she says is needed. What are the necessary ingredients? What conditions might be created to bring it about?

Theodore Roszak says in the opening paragraph of *The Making
of a Counter Culture:*

The struggle of the generations is one of the obvious constants of
human affairs. One stands in peril of some presumption, therefore,
to suggest that the rivalry between young and adult in Western
society during the current decade is uniquely critical. And yet
it is necessary to risk such presumption if one is not to lose sight
of our most important contemporary sources of radical dissent
and cultural innovation. For better or worse, most of what is
presently happening that is new, provocative, and engaging in
politics, education, the arts, social relations (love, courtship,
family, community), is the creation either of youth who are
profoundly, even fanatically, alienated from the parental generation, or of those who address themselves primarily to the young.
It is at the level of youth that significant social criticism now
looks for a responsive hearing as, more and more, it grows to
be the common expectation that the young should be those who
act, who make things happen, who take the risks, who generally
provide the ginger. It would be of interest in its own right that
the age-old process of generational disaffiliation should now be
transformed from a peripheral experience in the life of the

individual and the family into a major lever of radical social change. But if one believes, as I do, that the alienated young are giving shape to something that looks like the saving vision our endangered civilization requires, then there is no avoiding the need to understand and to educate them in what they are about.

Agree or disagree, substantiate or qualify, in response to this point of view. Speak from your own firsthand, personal experience of being young and knowing adults intimately and long.

10
Writing and the ultimate self

I decline to accept the end of man.
It is easy enough to say that man is
immortal simply because he will endure; that when the last ding-dong of
doom has clanged and faded from the
last worthless rock hanging tideless
in the last red and dying evening, that
even then there will still be one
more sound: that of his puny inexhaustible voice, still talking. I
refuse to accept this. I believe that
man will not merely endure: he will
prevail. He is immortal, not because
he alone among creatures has an inexhaustible voice, but because he has a
soul, a spirit capable of compassion
and sacrifice and endurance. The
poet's, the writer's, duty is to write
about these things. It is his privi-
lege to help man endure by lifting his
heart, by reminding him of the courage
and honor and hope and pride and compassion and pity and sacrifice which
have been the glory of his past. The
poet's voice need not merely be the
record of man, it can be one of the
props, the pillars to help him endure
and prevail.

WILLIAM FAULKNER, Nobel Prize Acceptance Speech

We live in an age when the human is being constantly diminished—rendered unimportant or irrelevant. The forces working to deprive people of their quality of *human*-ness are many and will increase in number and intensity in the decades ahead. In the past century, we have worked feverishly to bring the blessings of technology to the entire country and, in the process, have poisoned our lands, our water, our air. As the population has exploded and people have crowded into our great cities, the urban areas have become nightmares of hopelessness and despair, degradation and violence. Television and jet transports have contracted and compressed the world; they have also subtly diminished man's imaginative conception of himself. As life has become more computerized and homogenized, more comfortable and affluent, its meaning has become more trivial and elusive. People today live closer together, but exist farther apart. They have less cause for labor, but more reason for mental anguish. They have more of technocracy's abundance and wealth, but they have fewer of nature's simple gifts. They have gained in gewgaws and gadgetry, but they have lost in compassion and humanity.

In Faulkner's view, man will endure because he will continue to talk with his "puny inexhaustible voice." The image is a compelling one. And if, as Faulkner says, man will prevail because he has "a soul, a spirit capable of compassion and sacrifice and endurance," it will be because that soul and that spirit are given reality and made manifest by that "puny inexhaustible voice." The human voice is the bearer of the human spirit. To still it would be, in effect, to still humanity.

Now, more than ever before, is the time to sound the note of the human voice. If language itself becomes dehumanized, we lose the best hope of retaining our humanness.

The political rhetoric of our time has tended more and more to become dehumanized; the amount of public "doublespeak" increases dramatically. Phrases, sentences, and paragraphs appear to be machine-made rather than man-made. They result not from an individual's firsthand thinking and meditating and grappling with the complexities of reality and his or her own view of it, but from someone else's thinking, someone else's vocabulary, someone else's dogmas that have become rigidified and codified and sanctified at the same time as they have become dehumanized and even antihuman.

But politics is only one area of language use that has tended to become dehumanized. It is easy today to suffocate from, or at least to choke on, the great quantities of organization prose that surround us everywhere in our daily life—in government, in business, in universities, in industry.

In the midst of this contemporary madness, individuals must plant their feet firmly on the earth and speak forth in their individual voices with all the humanity they can summon. And they must, if they would preserve the human in human life, speak in their own language and nobody else's—certainly not in the language that is ground out by some machine or in the officialese of an organization or establishment. Those who speak in another's voice diminish not only themselves but all mankind.

Throughout history, the idea has appeared again and again in religions and philosophies that knowledge of the self becomes, in some sense, the ultimate knowledge, the highest wisdom attainable. The journey into the self is the most important journey any person can take; and it is taken, ironically, by staying at home, withdrawing into one's own being. In the middle of the nineteenth century, Walt Whitman began his journey this way in "Song of Myself":

I loafe and invite my soul,
I lean and loafe at my ease observing a spear of summer grass.
                    .   .   .
Creeds and schools in abeyance,
Retiring back a while sufficed at what they are, but never forgotten,
I harbor for good or bad, I permit to speak at every hazard,
Nature without check with original energy.

It is always the most familiar that is hardest to know. The self, so intimately familiar, is the hardest of all to know in any profound way.

Zen, it is said by Zen Buddhists, cannot be explained directly in words, but a great many stories, which have been passed down for many generations, are in the nature of anecdotes or parables and suggest the nature of Zen indirectly or obliquely. Here are two from *Zen Flesh, Zen Bones:*

"A Parable"
Buddha told a parable in a sutra:

A Man traveling across a field encountered a tiger. He fled, the tiger after him. Coming to a precipice, he caught hold of the root of a wild vine and swung himself down over the edge. The tiger sniffed at him from above. Trembling, the man looked down to where, far below, another tiger was waiting to eat him. Only the vine sustained him.

Two mice, one white and one black, little by little started to gnaw away the vine. The man saw a luscious strawberry near him. Grasping the vine with one hand, he plucked the strawberry with the other. How sweet it tasted!

"Open Your Own Treasure House"

Daiju visited the master Basō in China. Basō asked: "What do you seek?

"Enlightenment," replied Daiju.

"You have your own treasure house. Why do you search outside?" Basō asked.

Daiju inquired. "Where is my treasure house?"

Basō answered: "What you are asking is your treasure house."

Daiju was enlightened! Ever after he urged his friends: "Open your own treasure house and use those treasures."

Each of the principal characters in the two Zen stories comes in some sense to know "for the first time" the "place" where he "started."

> By knowing the Self . . . through
> hearing, reflection, and meditation,
> one comes to know all things. . . .
> As for water the one center is the
> ocean, as for touch the one center is
> the skin, as for smell the one center
> is the nose, as for taste the one
> center is the tongue, as for form the
> one center is the eyes, as for sound
> the one center is the ears, as for
> thought the one center is the mind,
> as for divine wisdom the one center is
> the heart—so for all beings the one
> center is the Self.
> "Brihararanyaka Upanishad"

Henry David Thoreau, author of *Walden,* is famous for having journeyed an immense distance by going only a short way away. He traveled out to the simple pond near his home town of Concord in 1845 and set up residence there for two years in a hut he built with his own hands, living largely off the produce of his own garden. He made clear his purpose in going to the pond when he wrote *Walden.*

> I went to the woods because I wished to live deliberately, to front only essential facts of life, and see if I could not learn what it had to teach, and not, when I came to die, discover that I had not lived. I did not wish to live what was not life, living is so dear; nor did I wish to practice resignation, unless it was quite necessary. I wanted to live deep and suck out all the marrow of life, to live so sturdily and Spartan-like as to put to rout all that was not life, to cut a broad swath and shave close, to drive life into a corner, and reduce it to its lowest terms, and if it proved to be mean, why then to get the whole and genuine meanness of it, and publish its meanness to the world; or if it were sublime, to know it by experience, and be able to give a true account of it in my next excursion.

Like the man pursued by the tiger, Thoreau wanted to have lived before he died; and like the man seeking enlightenment, he turned his search toward his own "treasure house" within.

Whitman, the characters in the Zen stories, and Thoreau, set off in quest of something we are all searching for, what is sometimes called the meaning of life, the reason for being, or the purpose of existence. These terms may sound impossibly vague, and concern for them is too often brushed aside by realists as sophomoric. But the concept of "the search for self" persists and returns to haunt even those who refuse to recognize it. There is surely no person who ever lived who did not wonder, at some time during his or her life, what life was all about. Different people might well have phrased the question differently, and the more sophisticated person might have disguised the simplicity and baldness of the question. No matter how it is phrased, the question basically nags us all.

The truth is that we answer the question for ourselves by the way we decide to live our lives. If we launch out on a ruthless pursuit of wealth or a mindless pursuit of pleasure, we have decided, consciously or unconsciously, what life is all about for us. In terms of existential philosophy, we define our "self" through our actions—the way we respond to events and actions, the way we act to reflect our instincts and beliefs.

What does this have to do with writing? As we have tried to suggest, the ultimate self that awaits discovery is shaped by us at the same time that it gives shape to our beings and our lives. The encounter is likely to be surrounded by silence, but it is invariably tied up with language, which we use constantly to explore and extend our understanding of self.

> Every time a poem is written, every
> time a short story is written, it is
> written not by cunning, but by belief.
> The beauty, the something, the little
> charm of the thing to be, is always
> more felt than known. There is a
> common jest, one that always annoys
> me, on the writers, that they write
> the last end first, and then work up
> to it; that they lay a train toward
> one sentence that they think is pretty
> nice and have all fixed up to set like
> a trap to close with. No, it should
> not be that way at all. No one who
> has ever come close to the arts has
> failed to see the difference between
> things written that way, with cunning
> and device, and the kind that are
> believed into existence, that begin
> in something more felt than known.
>
> ROBERT FROST
> "Education by Poetry: A Meditative Monologue"

The best writing that you—or any person—will do is writing that grows from genuine encounters with the self: writing, as Frost suggests, that is "believed into existence." Language may not be able to contain the essence of the encounter, but it is inevitably useful and even indispensable in making the preparation and in elaborating the consequences. Moreover, words can work wonderfully in oblique ways, as the Zen stories show about a philosophy that escapes the traps of all words, and as the mysteries and discoveries of your own writing reveal. We can use language to deepen the silences.

DISCUSSION

What is the fate of the individual in society these days? Can the individual voice be heard? What examples do you have to support or disprove Faulkner's assertion that humanity will "endure and prevail"?

Do you see evidence that the use of depersonalized language dehumanizes? Save and share some of the examples of dehumanized writing that you find or encounter.

Why is the self so mysterious and difficult to know? Why is it that people and groups as widely diverse as Zen Buddhists, Henry David Thoreau, and Walt Whitman engage in the search for self so intensely?

Have you had the experience in writing, described by Robert Frost, of creating something that begins "more felt than known"?

WRITING IDEAS AND EXPERIMENTS

Create some parables on the model of Zen parables that illustrate your basic attitudes and values toward life.

Put yourself metaphorically in the place of the gentleman clinging to the mouse-gnawed vine while a tiger waits above. What are some of the things you would want to do in your last moments? Or do them, and write about it.

What do you take to be—very tentatively—your ultimate self? Write a character sketch of yourself in which you try to get in touch with your deepest feelings about yourself.

Write an essay about a topic you have never really been willing to discuss or share previously. Bring to the surface something that is an important part of your ultimate self, yet with which you haven't been totally willing to deal.

Each of us has had moments of deep insight into the ultimate self—moments of joy and wonder and discovery when things seem to come together, to fit, and the unclear suddenly seems clear. Recall a moment of that kind from your own life and describe it.

FURTHER POINTS OF DEPARTURE

If you have been following this book more or less in order, you have written much and received reactions to your writing. Presumably you feel a good deal more comfortable about the way you write (and think and feel). For your "Rhetoric of the Imagination," write an informal essay recapturing the stages through which you have progressed in your writing. What pleases you most about your writing? What still causes problems? What can you do, what *will* you do to continue to grow as a person and a writer?

We have suggested a number of writing topics in this book. Now it's your turn. Write a list of ten or fifteen writing "assignments" for yourself—things you really want to write about, things from your ultimate self that you really should say.

The great novels, the great books, all deal in one way or another, with searches for the ultimate self. We will not offer a list of great books, but we suggest that you consider, in your reading, the theme of the search for the ultimate self—the problem of self-recognition, the difficulties of pursuing and finding and knowing the ultimate self.

II

extensions:
words in
the world

INTRODUCTION: LANGUAGE AND EXPERIENCE

Man is said to have language by nature. It is held that man, in distinction from plant and animal, is the only living being capable of speech. This statement does not mean only that, along with other faculties, man also possesses the faculty of speech. It means to say that only speech enables man to be the living being he is as man. It is as one who speaks that man is—man.

MARTIN HEIDEGGER, "Language"

Johnny Hart, *Hey! B.C.* Copyright © 1958, 1959 by the New York Herald Tribune, Inc. New York: Funk and Wagnalls.

"Language," it has been said, "is what makes us human" in contrast to other animals. Language makes up the raw materials of the writer, and after immersing yourself in the writing process in the first half of this book, it is appropriate to consider in some depth the nature of those materials. The next chapters of *Writing in Reality* explore the ways language interpenetrates our lives and affects and shapes our experience. This part of the book has been designed to help you develop a consciousness of the complexity of language, a sensitivity to the ambiguity of words, and an awareness of the intimate relation of your language to your experience. Although much of the material will be theoretical, the intent is very much practical: to provoke you into seeing, experiencing, and using what has probably become, through familiarity, unnoticed or invisible to you—words in the world.

What *is* language? It must be candidly admitted that there is no universally accepted definition. The linguistic scientist sees language as an immensely fascinating grammatical puzzle which can be observed, examined, and analyzed in a number of ways. A child in the seventh grade, on the other hand, may see language as "a bunch of rules," and pronounce this definition with suspicion and a grimace. There are books that will tell you that language is "a means for communication of ideas" or "a system of symbols used to convey thought." Others will describe language as a set of transformations and operations which allows humans to create original utterances. Still others will define language in terms of meaning and logic or dip into the jargon of electronics and communications theory to dwell on the notions of *sender, receiver, content,* and *feedback.*

The problem with these and other definitions is that they tend to treat a part, rather than the whole. They are like the definition of "man" supplied by a professor of anatomy: "Man is made up of a complex set of interrelated muscles, organs, and bones, which serve to enable him to grow and reproduce himself." We might well ask, "Is that all?" What has happened to the living breathing creature with a soul—you or me?

By . . . various mechanisms . . .
great masses of nerve cells—the brain
is a great unity—act together; and
not merely do two or a billion units
sum their separate contributions, but
each is a part of a dynamic fluctuat-
ing activity pattern of the whole.
This is the orchestra which plays
thoughts of truth and beauty, which
creates creative imagination.

R. W. GERARD, "The Biological Basis of Imagination"

The best way to shake a limited view from one's mind is to stand back deliberately from the rush of experience and watch the way language permeates all life. We notice, of course, that language is used to describe experience—as we tell tales and, in turn, listen to stories about what happened. But we quickly see, too, that language not only describes experience, it *actually exists as a part of experience.* When you say something or hear something, the language itself becomes a part of the situation or incident. Language is not removed from life or independent of it; it is an inseparable part of life.

We literally live in, by, and with language. When we wake, we are bombarded with radio or television news and chatter, and we mutter back our reactions as we prepare ourselves for another day of encounter with the world—an encounter that will take place largely *through* language. Over breakfast we scan the newspaper and keep up a run-ning stream of internal linguistic response—*oh, another automobile wreck at the intersection, the strike negotiations are getting nowhere, the president is going to veto a money bill but Congress will probably override the veto, the stock-market fell again, and the Tigers dropped two at Boston, oh, there was a murder just a few blocks away, I wonder . . .* The stream of private language is occasionally broken by utterances aloud to a companion or acquaintance. As the day progresses, our language will loosen and flow freely, sound-ing out the world, reaching out to a friend, defending against a foe, cajoling a girlfriend, boyfriend or spouse, con-veying feelings, concealing emotions, exploring meaning, trying out ideas, hiding intentions, and on and on and on, moving through and shaping the world: holding it off, letting it in, trying it out, turning it off, down, or up.

This linguistic encounter with the world is by no means one way. Accompanying the outflow is the constant inflow —a stream of language from the outside to the inside— through ear and eye, as we listen and read our way through life. As we sit in a restaurant over coffee with friends engaged in a discussion of campus politics, we hear a radio in the corner blaring the casualty figures in the most recent catastrophe; we glance at the headlines of a newspaper on the table; we look at ingredients listed on a ketchup bottle label; we note the warning to get a check-up for lung cancer on the back of a matchbook; we read a billboard down the street promoting a brand of cigarettes while telling us that cigarettes will kill us; we hear stray words from many conversations; we tune in briefly to a whispered quarrel at a nearby table; we flip through a paperback that we bought on impulse at a newsstand.

The dictionaries still say that "language is a device for communicating ideas." The semanticists and the anthropologists agree that this is a tiny, specialized function of speech. Mainly, language is an instrument for action. The meaning of a word or phrase is not its dictionary equivalent but the difference its utterance brings about in a situation. We use words to comfort and cajole ourselves in fantasy and daydream, to let off steam, to goad ourselves into one type of activity and to deny ourselves another. We use words to promote our own purposes in dealing with others. We build up verbal pictures of ourselves and our motives. We coax, wheedle, protest, invite, and threaten. Even the most intellectual of intellectuals employs only a minute fraction of his total utterance in symbolizing and communicating ideas that

are divorced from emotion and action.
The primary social value of speech
lies in getting individuals to work
more effectively together and in easing
social tensions. Very often what is
said matters much less than that
something is said.

CLYDE KLUCKHOHN, *Mirror for Man*

We live as surrounded by language as by air, taking it
in and releasing it as naturally as we inhale and exhale. We
are bombarded on every side, assaulted every hour by language demanding, commanding, attention. We are forced
to pick and choose; to tune in or tune out; to see and read or
turn and depart; to say "yes," "no," or "maybe"; to argue,
agree, or remain suspended in doubt. We thread our way
through the maze of many tongues; we make money and we
make love; we encounter the world and shape it as it shapes
us; we know life as it comes to know us—all through
words, words, words.

Language, then, is far more than a medium of communication; it is indeed a kind of *creation*. With it we make
our world and ourselves. Through our daily linguistic encounter with the world, we proclaim our identities, shape
our lives, and (in some small or big way) leave our impress
on the world.

One might legitimately ask: "If language is so terribly
complex and terribly difficult to define, what is the point in
exploring or trying to understand it?" Indeed, some people
find that when they think consciously about language—
especially their own—the flow of words dries up completely;
they are unable to think or write because they are inhibited
by formal considerations.

We certainly do not intend to create such a problem;
however, we do see great value in "consciousness raising"
about the nature of language and meaning at this point.
Perhaps a brief anecdote will make the reason apparent:

A few years ago, while returning from a professional
convention of English teachers, one of us witnessed a confrontation between two passengers who had attended the
conference and an airline stewardess. The two people had

requested seats in the nonsmoking section of the plane, and the ticket agent had actually assigned them the first two seats directly behind that area, which was designated by a little plastic card pinned to a seat.

The stewardess could have resolved the problem simply by moving the card back one row, but even that was not necessary. By virtue of their being nonsmokers, the two had effectively extended the nonsmoking section by occupying the seats immediately behind the area.

Obviously both the stewardess and the two people were hopelessly word bound. A sign, with arbitrary symbols printed on plastic, created a barrier to thinking which they could not overcome. The argument continued, and finally the stewardess negotiated with other passengers and moved the two inside the "officially designated" nonsmoking boundaries.

Ironically, one of the two English teachers involved in the dispute was carrying a book entitled *The Awareness of Meaning.*

People do need to be aware of meanings to avoid being linguistically trapped. In the chapters that follow, we will present some basic discussion of such areas as how words acquire meaning, how we create through language, the relationship between language and logic, the role of nonprint languages in our lives. Some reflections and experiments are included to encourage you to become more deeply conscious of the linguistic environment in which you live and to develop an *awareness of meaning* that carries beyond the pages of a book.

DISCUSSION

What is your definition of language? What does language represent to you? Are you conscious of your own use of language?

Think about a single episode during a recent day—a coffee break, lunch, a debate, or conversation—and describe the different linguistic elements which enter. Recall, and try to account for, the course of the conversation. How did the talk move from topic to topic? Why? Was the direction shaped by language, or did it shape the language, or both?

Try to remember examples of "language blindness" you have witnessed. How often do you encounter people whose lack of awareness of meaning limits their effectiveness, who act, for instance, as if words, signs, orders, and instructions were fixed and real rather than symbols?

IDEAS AND EXPERIMENTS[1]

Keep a running account of your own use of, and encounters with, language for one day. Consider how much time you spend in various language activities: communicating ideas, absorbing ideas, expressing emotions, exploring facts, etc.

Keep a log of the many kinds of language that you use—both as "sender" and "receiver"—during a day or a half day. Make a list of the language forms and media—chat, poetry, essay, billboard, radio, lecture—that you are involved with and which thus create part of your life.

Pick a single common word—*dog, cat, football*—and spend ten or fifteen minutes listing all the associations the word has for you. How much data in your mind is linked to a single word?

FURTHER POINTS OF DEPARTURE

In a seminal book called *The Silent Language* (Doubleday, 1959) anthropologist Edward Hall argued that the ways in which people use space and time within a culture carry certain messages and meanings, few of which are conscious, creating a "silent language." Read Hall's book (or his later discussion of silent language, *The Hidden Dimension*) to explore additional ways in which language permeates our lives.

Hidden languages abound in our lives. For instance, in the silent language of architecture, structures we build say things about who and what we are. Make a study of the architecture of your own campus or city to see what various eras had to say. Study the hidden languages of automobiles, hamburger stands, consumer packaging, typography (what are the type faces of this book intended to convey?), book jackets, or any of the other silent languages you can identify.

---

[1] In Part Two we will drop the word "writing" and refer only to "Ideas and Experiments." Some of the activities will ask you to write informal essays or keep notes, but others will emphasize observing and responding in other ways.

11

How language means

The "meaning of meaning" is a topic that invariably puzzles and perplexes; it has probably been debated almost as long as man has had language with which to make meaning. Indeed, the whole question of how meaning came into existence at all is a fascinating topic, and linguists and anthropologists have written volumes sketching out theories of the origin of language. Various theories of language have been developed. The "Bow-Wow" theory holds that people learned to speak by imitating sounds in nature; the "Yo-He-Ho" theory asserts that language evolved from group chants during heavy labor; the "Goo-Goo" theory claims that speech evolved as infants' babbling was reinforced by their mothers.

Just as the origin of language in human history fascinates, so does the process of language acquisition in young children. How is it that a baby learns to sort out events and experiences, sights and sounds, so that at a very young age he or she can associate particular sounds and experiences consistently in a way that indicates an ability to "make meaning"?

Also puzzling is the relationship between meaning and reality. Is something so because we say it is so? Is there any correspondence between what we say things are and what they really are, and if so, what is the connection? Does attaching a label to something—*teapot, love*—stabilize its nature?

However unclear the meaning of meaning may be, the thinking of linguists and philosophers on the topic has changed considerably within the last century. Until quite recently, meaning and language were seen as somehow changeless—set according to universal standards. In the preface to *A Dictionary of the English Language* (1755), Samuel Johnson could lament the inevitable decline and decay of these standards:

> Those who have been persuaded to think well of my design, require that it [the *Dictionary*] should fix our language, and put a stop to those alterations which time and chance have hitherto been suffered to make in it without opposition. With this consequence I will confess that I flattered myself for a while; but now begin to fear that I have indulged expectation which neither reason nor experience can justify. When we see men grow old and die at a certain time one after another, from century to century, we laugh at the elixir that promises to prolong life to a thousand years; and with equal justice may the lexicographer be derided, who being able to produce no example of a nation that has preserved their words and phrases from mutability, shall imagine that his dictionary can embalm his language, and secure it from corruption and decay, that it is in his power to change sublunary nature, or clear the world at once from folly, vanity, and affectation.

Though Johnson lamented the decline, he did his best to prevent it:

> If the changes that we fear be thus irresistible, what remains but to acquiesce with silence, as in the other insurmountable distresses of humanity? It remains that we retard what we cannot repel, that we palliate what we cannot cure. Life may be lengthened by care, though death cannot be ultimately defeated: tongues, like governments, have a natural tendency to degeneration; we have long preserved our constitution, let us make some struggles for our language.
>
>   In hope of giving longevity to that which its own nature forbids to be immortal, I have devoted this book, the labour of years, to the honour of my country, that we may no longer yield the palm of philology to the nations of the continent.

His dictionary entries frequently—and often arbitrarily—legislated proper and improper language behavior and usage.

   But language has a way of escaping anyone's rules or laws, and as we have come to realize, the human use of language bubbles along, oblivious to philosopher's and dictionary-maker's objections or advice. Change in language does not invariably reflect decay. In this century, people have given up their search for an inflexible adherence of word to world, of language to observable objects and facts; they have begun to see language as a vital, living, changing, adaptable set of usages, customs, or practices that serve a multitude of human purposes. We see now that the meaning of a word lies not outside language, but inside it, in the way it is used.

Compare the following statement on language usage (from the Third Edition of *Webster's New International Dictionary*) to the quotation from Samuel Johnson:

The entry, definition, and proper classification of selected nonstandard and substandard English words have been greatly extended in the New Edition. . . . With the growth in literacy of the past century, and the increase, in fiction and drama, in radio and motion picture, of the use of dialect, slang, and colloquial speech, it has become necessary for a general dictionary to record and interpret the vocabularies of geographical and occupational dialects, and of the livelier levels of the speech of the educated. The shifting status of many expressions in slang and colloquial speech has made it necessary to review and rejudge the status and validity of all such terms, whether newly collected or contained in former editions of this Dictionary. Slang terms and slang meanings of standard words have been entered only when there is evidence that the slang term has been in use for a considerable length of time, and when it has been used in a printed work which is likely to continue being read.

In our time, then, dictionary makers and linguists are no longer concerned with legislating manners and morals through language; they are more interested in discovering and describing the richness of language than in applying status labels to particular uses.

"When I use a word, "Humpty Dumpty said, in rather a scornful tone, "it means just what I choose it to mean— neither more nor less."

"The question is," said Alice, "whether you can make words mean so many different things."

"The question is," said Humpty Dumpty, "which is to be master—that's all."
LEWIS CARROLL, *Through the Looking-Glass*

The problem of meaning persists and will no doubt continue to persist as long as language lasts; it is inherent in the nature of language. There will always be those who insist, in a literal-minded way, that words mean what the dictionary says they mean, nothing more and nothing less; and there will always be those who, like Humpty Dumpty, insist that words mean whatever they choose to have them mean. Indeed, just a decade and a half ago, when the new *Webster's International* did not label "ain't" an "improper" or "illiterate" usage, it was savagely attacked by the popular press and was itself labeled "cheap" and "corrupt," allegedly contributing to the death of meaning.

What is clear is that words acquire meaning through use over the years, and these meanings are collected in the dictionaries. But it is important to emphasize that meaning accrues through *use*. The dictionary, then, is not a final authority; the final authority is a body of language users. Language is in a constant state of change, and all that dictionaries can do is follow not make the changes.

> . . . the ideas with which we deal in our apparently disciplined waking life are by no means as precise as we like to believe. On the contrary, their meaning (and their emotional significance for us) becomes more imprecise the more closely we examine them. The reason for this is that anything we have heard or experienced can become sublimal—that is to say, can pass into the unconscious. And even what we retain in our conscious mind and can reproduce at will has acquired an unconscious undertone that will color the idea each time it is recalled.
> . . . Even the most carefully defined philosophical or mathematical concept, which we are sure does not contain more than we have put into it, is nevertheless more than we assume. It is a psychic event and as such partly unknowable. The very numbers you use in counting are more than you take them to be. They are at the same time mythological elements (for the

Pythagoreans, they were even divine);
but you are certainly unaware of this
when you use numbers for a practical
purpose.

Every concept in our conscious mind,
in short, has its own psychic associations. While such associations may
vary in intensity (according to the
relative importance of the concept to
our whole personality, or according to
the other ideas and even complexes to
which it is associated in our unconscious), they are capable of changing
the "normal" character of that concept. It may become something quite
different as it drifts below the level
of unconsciousness.

CARL G. JUNG, *Man and His Symbols*

But even to discuss meanings in terms of dictionary definitions is too simple, dictionaries necessarily ignore the most important aspect of words: that words have specific meanings for
particular people. Perhaps the best way of understanding this
idea is to use Jung's idea of words as "psychic events" for both
speaker and hearer, writer and reader. Words emerge from the
depths of one mind, dripping with associations; they are sent out
into the world, caught, and plunged again into the depths of
another mind, where there may be shock waves or stillness, de-
pending on the receiver's previous experience. Each attempt at
communication is a psychic event, unpredictable by the sender
of the language.

As John Steinbeck implies, the meaning of a word—or phrase,
clause, paragraph, secret, or story—is to be found in both speaker
and listener:

A man who tells secrets or stories must think of who is hearing or
reading, for a story has as many versions as it has readers. Everyone
takes what he wants or can from it and thus changes it to his measure.
Some pick out parts and reject the rest, some strain the story through
their mesh of prejudice, some paint it with their own delight. A
story must have some points of contact with the reader to make
him feel at home in it.

JOHN STEINBECK, *The Winter of Our Discontent*

There are many more stories than the one that appears on a printed page.

It is also the psychic nature of words and meaning that creates the mystery and magic of poetry and poetic language:

Words in a poem, sounds in movement, rhythm in space, attempt to recapture personal meaning in personal time and space from out of the sights and sounds of a depersonalized, dehumanized world. They are bridgeheads into alien territory. They are acts of insurrection. Their source is from the Silence at the center of each of us. Wherever and whenever such a whorl of patterned sound or space is established in the external world, the power that it contains generates new lines of force whose effects are felt for centuries.

The creative breath "comes from a zone of man where man cannot descend, even if Virgil were to lead him, for Virgil would not go down there."

R. D. LAING, *The Politics of Experience*

The poet is always struggling, not to make new language, but to make language new—to capture surprise and wonder and mystery in new arrangements and new uses of words. He or she is critically dependent on this magic dimension, searching for the tone, the language, that will set up vibrations deep within the readers. Emily Dickinson has described the poet thus:

This was a Poet—It is That
Distills amazing sense
From ordinary Meanings—
And Attar so immense

From the familiar species
That perished by the Door—
We wonder it was not Ourselves
Arrested it—before.

EMILY DICKINSON, "This was a Poet"

The poet has an acute awareness of many meanings of words and deals with them—takes calculated risks with them—as a matter of course in the writing of poems.

It must be remembered that the words in poems and the words in prose are the same. The prose writer, too, often derives "amazing sense" from "ordinary meanings," and the individual response to words and phrases is not likely to be altered much by whether the words are set in lines or in paragraphs. Whether producing poetry or prose, the writer takes calculated risks with the meanings of words. The keener the calculation, the more effective he or she is likely to be in achieving success in writing.

An awareness of words as psychic events is equally important in the world of functional discourse. Semanticist Alfred Korzybski pointed out that too many people act as if words were things— real objects—rather than symbols which evoke dramatically different responses from different people. As a result, discussions often drift aimlessly, lacking center and focus; words that were meant to soothe, enrage; nations go to war for vague abstractions, understood only dimly by the combatants; and tyrants can enflame mobs and manipulate people irrationally. As Korzybski argued, an enormous amount of confusion, misunderstanding, and hate could be eliminated if sender and receiver simply recognized that meanings vary—that words are psychic events.

DISCUSSION

Use your understanding of the meaning of meaning to study the way discussions go awry. How often do class or individual discussions lose focus because participants are talking about different concerns but using the same words. How can group discussions be enhanced by informal definition of terms?

Bring in something you have written much earlier in the course, putting as much distance as possible between you and the piece of writing. Investigate the ambiguities that appear to you now that did not when you wrote the piece. How can you go about clearing them up? Try the piece out on some friends, and find out how they interpret it. Where there are differences between their interpretation and your intention, investigate the causes.

When you were a child, you may have had impressions or feelings about big words you didn't understand. You knew that a parent worked in a "chemical plant" but had only a dim vision of what this piece of foliage might resemble, or you visualized a "disciplinarian" as a great big bird. Resurrect some of those meanings and discuss how they originated.

Observe your own reaction to words, phrases, and sentences and give an account of instances in which you have made the language mean something different from the intention of the speaker or writer. Probe your background and discover, where you can, what caused you to bring a different meaning to the language than that intended.

Meanings differ. Choose a common word and explore how individual definitions differ. First, look up a common definition in a dictionary; then describe the personal meanings the word has for you based on your own experience. Finally compare your meanings with those of other people.

IDEAS AND EXPERIMENTS

Dictionary making proceeds through a process of collecting examples of a word in use—citations—and constructing a definition based on current usage. Choose a common word—*run, walk, sleep, car, ball,* etc.—collect citations, and construct a definition based solely on the evidence without drawing on your past associations. How close do you come to a dictionary definition? How many citations must you collect to create what you regard as an adequate definition?

Write two versions of a proposition, idea, or conviction in which you believe strongly, one stripped down to essentials and couched in terms as precise and exact as possible, another in which you exploit all the resonance of language in attempting to convey the complexity and subtlety of your proposition to your reader—perhaps even persuading him or her that the proposition is true.

Write an essay or story in which you use a number of invented words and provide your reader with the context for understanding their meaning without being specifically told what they mean.

Choose a word (or phrase) that is rich in personal associations for you—*prom, father, swimming pool, bacon,* etc.—and write a narrative or short story that describes the origin of your personal definition.

Collect from your personal experience some examples of times when people (or yourself) have made language mean something different from the generally accepted meaning. Or try out a few words or phrases and write an account of the reaction.

FURTHER POINTS OF DEPARTURE

Find examples from the newspapers of incidents or clashes caused by senders and receivers having made language mean different things.

A number of "popular," nontechnical descriptions of the origins of language and the history of the English language have been written. Find a good, readable book and study the ways in which language has taken on meaning.

Read Lewis Carroll's "Jabberwocky," a nonsense poem in *Through the Looking-Glass*, that actually makes a kind of sense. Consider the ways in which strange, unfamiliar, or unknown words can take on meaning through their location in sentences and the meanings of words surrounding them.

Read the introductory matter in *Webster's New International Dictionary,* Third Edition, and write a report on its attitudes toward change in language. What does Webster's have to say about the nature of "good English" and changing usage habits?

Creating order out of chaos

> The relation of thought to word is not a thing but a process, a continual movement back and forth from thought to word and from word to thought. In that process the relation of thought to word undergoes changes which themselves may be regarded as development in the functional sense. Thought is not merely expressed in words; it comes into existence through them. Every thought tends to connect something with something else, to establish a relationship between things.
>
> L. S. VYGOTSKY, *Thought and Language*

"How do I know what I mean until I see what I said?" This exclamation—common enough—suggests a problem that has puzzled people for a long time: What is the relationship between saying and thinking, between language and thought? Looked at in one way, language appears to be simply the clothing of naked thought, a way of dressing up and presenting one's ideas. But as we have suggested, language and thinking are closely interrelated—inseparable, in fact—for a particular thought expressed in particular words cannot be expressed in any other words without subtly changing meaning and impact.

> The structure of speech does not simply mirror the structure of thought; that is why words cannot be put on by

> thought like a ready-made garment.
> Thought undergoes many changes as it
> turns into speech. It does not merely
> find expression in speech; it finds
> its reality and form.
>
> L. S. VYGOTSKY, *Thought and Language*

Further, using language is enormously important in helping people *order* their experience. Life is infinitely more complex than simple persons, places, or things. We are constantly bombarded with sensory impressions, and we use language to order —indeed, to defend against—this complexity. If we were forced to cope separately with each of our experiences during a single day, we would promptly go mad. To avoid being swamped by this random flux and flow of experience, we create linguistic order out of the chaos of experience. As William James suggests, we break our experience into "ten thousand separate serial orders," each of which can be considered, contemplated, or acted on separately.

The real world as it is given objectively at this moment is the sum total of all its beings and events now. But can we think of such a sum? Can we realize for an instant what a cross-section of all existence at a definite point of time would be? While I talk and the flies buzz, a sea gull catches a fish at the mouth of the Amazon, a tree falls in the Adirondack wilderness, a man sneezes in Germany, a horse dies in Tartary, and twins are born in France. What does it mean? Does the contemporaneity of these events with one another, and with a million others as disjointed, form a rational bond between them, and unite them into anything that means for us a world? Yet just such a collateral contemporaneity, and nothing else, is the real order of the world. It is an order with which we have nothing to do but to get away from it as fast as possible. As I said, we break it: we break it into histories, and we break it into arts, and we break it into sciences; and then we begin to feel at home. We make ten thousand separate serial orders of it, and on any one of these we react as though the others did not exist.

WILLIAM JAMES, *The Will to Believe*

Suzanne Langer has argued that human beings are, above all, symbol-making creatures. A symbol is an abstraction, which represents one or several experiences. Some symbols are quite specific in their representation—*key, kick, razor*—while others represent broad categories of experience—*love, hate, freedom, truth.* Every symbol—every word—grows in meaning through abstractions from experience: things and elements thrown together in classes and groups; subtle or minute distinctions glossed over to get at essences; complex ideas transformed into simple ones through selection of main features, principal aspects, or dominant traits.

> I believe there is a primary need in
> man. . . . This basic need, which
> certainly is obvious only in man, is
> the need of symbolization. The symbol-
> making function is one of man's
> primary activities, like eating, look-
> ing, or moving about. It is the
> fundamental process of his mind, and
> goes on all the time. Sometimes we
> are aware of it, sometimes we merely
> find its results, and realize that
> certain experiences have passed through
> our brains and have been digested
> there.
>
> SUZANNE LANGER, *Philosophy in a New Key*

We walk into the woods by a pond on a sunny, summer day, and the details of the landscape that clamor for the attention of the senses of sight, smell, touch are so many as to be beyond count—their subtle shadings requiring a lifetime or more to measure and record—but we say simply, "What a beautiful day! Look at that blue sky, that water . . . the trees." We attempt to suggest symbolically—in language—something of the nature of the total experience of the woods on a particular occasion by a severe selection of a few dominant features. As experience becomes more complicated than a simple stroll through the woods, the challenge to grasp and convey something of its nature in language becomes even greater.

In the process of abstracting, however, something is also lost; though we gain the ability to synthesize and manage our universe, we also lose specific details, for as one abstracts, the uncommon elements of an experience will often be ignored. While abstracting is an important way for us to order the chaos around us, the danger in abstracting is that one can lose touch with the fine details of experience.

Much poetry, in fact, is devoted to discovery—rediscovery—of the uncommon in the everyday. William Carlos Williams writes:

so much depends
upon

a red wheel
barrow

glazed with rain
water

beside the white
chickens

WILLIAM CARLOS WILLIAMS
"The Red Wheelbarrow"

Clearly a complex process of thinking/seeing/feeling/abstracting lies beneath this simple poem. "So much depends. . . ." What depends? We don't really know, but we can see that, through the symbol-making process, Williams has carefully selected details which lead the reader toward experiencing and recovering some of the poet's feelings

The relationships of thought to language to experience are complicated. The exclamation: "How do I know what I mean until I see what I said?" recognizes this complexity. But we might add: "Even when I see what I said, I may have to dig beneath the words to find what I mean." Thought and language and experience flow together in an interconnected process. Thought is a spur to language, and language, in turn, becomes a spur to thought; both combine in a gradual development of an elaborate structure of experience. Thought without language remains blunt and gross; language without thought remains inert and dead. Without either, experience remains unperceived or unstructured. Brought together in the right relationship, thought breathes life into language, while language grants grace, shape, form, and subtlety to thought.

This, in turn, suggests that the process of reasoning is vastly more complex than many have imagined. "Be logical," we are told; "be reasonable." Yet because of the interplay of language, perception, thinking, and feeling, being logical is not as easy as it sounds.

From time immemorial, some philosophers (and many human beings on occasion) have speculated about and wished for a world controlled by logic, a world where emotional responses would be banned from the mind and all disputes settled by "sweet reason." The Greek philosophers developed the *syllogism*—the classical formula of deductive logic—which begins with a major premise (*All men are mortal*), followed by a minor premise (*Socrates is a man*), and clinched by a conclusion (*Therefore, Socrates is mortal*). The neatness, tidiness, and simplicity have some appeal, for at first glance, they frequently seem the means to the creation of a utopia where reason might reign.

But logical formulae disappoint deeply. When one moves from such systems to the street, a strange thing happens: The world seems indifferent to their classic simplicity, unamenable to their directness, and impatient with their irrelevance. No person has ever been known to decide whether or not to drop a hot bowl, or whom to marry, or which presidential candidate to vote for through the use of a series of syllogisms. Arguments are carried on hotly without reference to forms of logic, and people who try to introduce them may find themselves despised or ignored.

> Aristotelian logic suggests that if something is "good," it must be "all good" . . . ; that that which is "not good" must be "bad" . . . ; and that nothing can be "good" and "bad" at the same time. . . . In real life, however, good and bad are usually mixed, and it is seldom possible to impose such simplistic categories on experience. The difficulty with Aristotle's "laws of logic" is that while they <u>seem</u> sensible, in fact they are inadequate to deal with reality, forcing us to press it into narrow confines.
>
> s. i. HAYAKAWA, *Language in Thought and Action*

In contrast, then, to the simplistic, depersonalized syllogisms of the logician (Figure 12–1), a more accurate approximation of the process of reason would look like a complex web with a real human being at the center. Our attempt (also simplistic, of course) is shown in Figure 12–2. Faced with a problem or decision, the real world decision maker draws on a rich variety of resources in a complex process that can be called "reason." For instance, instead of relying on broad, two-valued premises, the

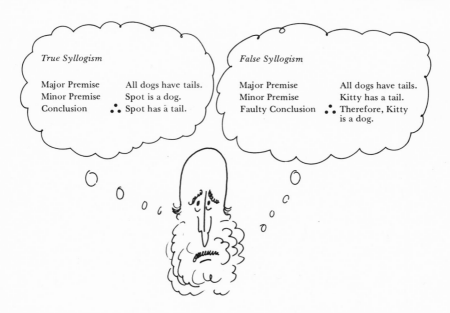

Figure 12–1   Syllogisms. Of the two syllogisms above, one leads to a false conclusion because of a violation of the "laws" of logic which dictate that the same term ("tail") cannot appear as the direct object of both major and minor premises. Classical logic is filled with discussion of patterns for proper and improper syllogisms. Whether true or false, the conclusions drawn by syllogisms were frequently trivial and simplistic. (What happens to the "true" syllogism if Spot has had his tail bobbed?)

real person bases decisions on a complex, subtle set of beliefs, attitudes, and values (the person is only half aware of them). Where did these values come from? Dozens of places: from past experiences, from early childhood training, from parents and friends and enemies and public figures and associates, and from reading and writing and thinking. The person also draws, not on universal principles and axioms, but on a storehouse of individual experiences, experiences from a childhood in Connecticut or Arizona, on particular experiences with particular friends. The reasoner also uses intuition and insight and flash inspiration. Even then, no decision is made solely in the abstract, for any decision is set in a context of current circumstances. No decision can be made without consideration of the present circumstances, of avenues that are possible or impossible, desirable or undesirable, practical or impractical, consequential or inconsequential.

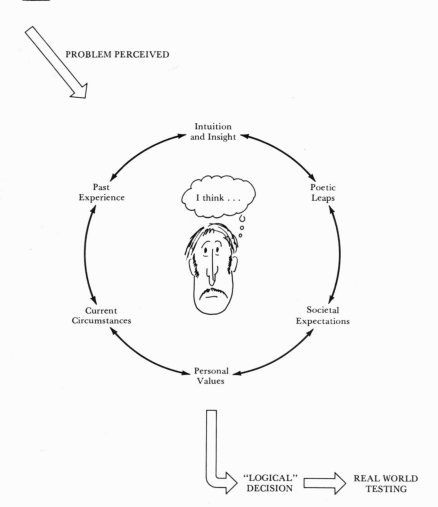

PROBLEM PERCEIVED

Figure 12–2

Our real world thinker, then, balances assumption, insights, values, circumstances, and experiences, weighs them, mulls them over, and somehow—through a process not understood by Greek philosophers or a brain surgeon—reaches a decision. R. W. Gerard calls this process, "imagination":

Imagination is one manifestation or index of how the brain machine works, which in turn depends on how it is built. And since sensory data are shaped by such reworking, imagination pervades all thought and knowledge.

R. W. GERARD, "The Biological Basis of Imagination"

A twentieth-century poet put it this way:

The truth seems to be that we live in concepts of the imagination before the reason has established them. If this is true, then reason is simply the methodizer of the imagination.

WALLACE STEVENS, "Imagination Value"

R. W. Gerard continues:

Imagination, not reason, creates the novel. It is to social inheritance what mutation is to biological inheritance; it accounts for the survival of the fittest. Reason or logic, applied when judgment indicates that the new is promising, acts like natural selection to pan the gold grains from the sand and insure the survival of the fittest. Imagination supplies the premises and asks the questions from which reason grinds out the conclusions as a calculating machine supplies answers.

Both Gerard and Stevens see imagination, not logic, at the heart of the process of creating order out of chaos and as a central factor in the interplay between experience and thought. Once again, that interplay is deeply based in language. We use language to structure and order our past experiences; we use language in the process of reaching a decision (both talking to ourselves and talking to others); and we use language to express that decision and to assess its effects.

DISCUSSION

Talk over all the words you can think of relating to reason—*horse sense, ratiocination, logic, analysis, mind, thought, brain*—and show how you might discriminate among them: What view of "sweet reason" does each support?

Discuss the relationship between language and thought in the following sayings taken from Benjamin Franklin's *Poor Richard's Almanac:*

If you would know the value of money, go and try to borrow some.
'Tis hard for an empty bag to stand upright.
Let thy maid-servant be faithful, strong, and homely.
Fish and visitors smell in three days.

> If you would have a faithful servant, and one that you like, serve yourself.

Discuss this statement by Martin Heidegger:

> Man acts as though he were the shaper and master of language, while in fact language remains the master of man. When this relation of dominance gets inverted, man hits upon strange maneuvers. Language becomes the means of expression. As expression, language can decay into mere medium for the printed word. That even in such employment of language we retain a concern for care in speaking is all to the good. But this alone will never help us to escape from the inversion of the true relation of dominance between language and man. Man first speaks when, and only when, he responds to language by listening to its appeal.

What is Heidegger saying about language and thought?

Discuss or debate informally a current social or political issue or problem—abortion, drug laws, the rights of prisoners, the elderly. Have a recorder keep track of the arguments which are presented and review his or her list. How many are based on pure reason? How many are sheer emotion? Are some arguments a blend of reason and emotion? Which are most effective?

IDEAS AND EXPERIMENTS

Sybil Marshall has commented that it is terribly difficult for adults to recall what it is like to be a child; and this is accurate, in part, because adults' symbol systems and their abstractions have become—with time—much more complex and abstract than they were in childhood (*An Experiment in Education,* Cambridge, 1963). Think back to your childhood to a particularly memorable event or scene, one that influenced you strongly. Try to recapture the moment in words. Then, think about your current understanding about what happened. How has your own ability to abstract through language increased your understanding of a long ago experience?

Take a ten minute stroll down a busy street recording—with notebook or possibly a tape recorder—as many sights and sounds as you can. How much data can you process? How much must be ignored? Then try to capture impressionistically what you have seen/heard/felt in a paragraph or poem.

Spend some time—a leisurely period—attempting to rediscover the familiar. Find a scene that you see or pass frequently but have come to accept without thought. Pause and describe it as fully as language will allow. Rediscover objects, elements, relationships, colors, textures, shapes, movements. Capture the scene in prose or poetry.

Write a satirical account of a person who decides to use logic and reason exclusively in selecting a person to marry, a car to buy, or a politician to support.

Put down on paper one of your pet prejudices or beliefs. After you have stated it simply, begin a process of self-probing to discover its origins, its nature, its consequences, and go as deep as you can in finding what lies beneath it. How did development of this prejudice evolve as an abstraction based on one (or several) experience?

Find an editorial in your daily paper and consider what appears to be the result of emotion, what of imagination, and what of reason. Rewrite the piece in strictly logical or strictly emotional terms. What happens?

FURTHER POINTS OF DEPARTURE

Read one of Edgar Allan Poe's "tales of ratiocination"—"The Murders in the Rue Morgue," "The Gold-Bug," or "The Purloined Letter"—and discuss the amount of reason as against the amount of imagination displayed by the characters in the story, and by Poe in writing the story. Or do the same for a Sherlock Holmes mystery, or a contemporary detective novel, perhaps something by Agatha Christie, Helen MacInness, Ross MacDonald, Virgil Scott, or Eric Ambler.

Look up two or more different translations of the same work and explore the effect of the differences. Is the basic thought altered in the various versions? Are subtleties of thought altered? If you know the original language, check the translations against the original work and discuss the difficulties faced by the translators.

Find or write a series of paraphrases of a poem or a paragraph of prose. Discuss the alterations of thought that come with the alteration of language.

13

Language play

POLONIUS What do you read, my lord?
HAMLET Words, words, words.

SHAKESPEARE, Hamlet

. . . what we are blind and deaf to
within ourselves, we are also blind
and deaf to in the outer world,
whether it be playfulness, poetic
feeling, aesthetic sensitivity, primary
creativity, or the like.

ABRAHAM H. MASLOW, Sign, Image, Symbol

Language has been taken so seriously for so long that many people think of language only in relation to the sober side of life. Language performs so many serious functions in society, including the burial and occasional resurrection of thought in large tomes that fill the shelves of libraries. Even in school, where reading and writing are the keys to success, language deficiencies are treated with the seriousness of a capital offense.

However, language is at least as closely allied to the playful side of life as to the sober. If we think of language in terms of play, we enter more deeply into its spirit and essence. Even so traditional and distinguished a philologist as Otto Jespersen believed that the "genesis of language is not to be sought in the prosaic, but in the poetic side of life." Although he was thinking primarily of the origin of language in the beginnings of time, what he said seems to have considerable truth for the generation of language in everyday use.

If we kept an account of our language use throughout a typical day, we would probably discover that we use language as much for simple fun as for communication of serious ideas. Most people find themselves more frequently on the poetic than on the prosaic side of life. When we are at our ease we use language in the sheer ebullience of good spirits—to express those good spirits —and thus create, unconsciously, poems in praise of existence. We use language to gossip and, without pretension or consciousness, create narratives, epics, and myths which lighten our lives, amuse us, or simply interest us and relieve the monotony of sustained, sober existence. We tell each other stories, jokes, anecdotes. We talk and we listen, we listen and we talk. All the time we are snatching fragments from the flow of enigmatic human experience and reducing it to manageable form and understandable proportions, frequently spiced with a bit of humor.

> One of the things that is a very interesting thing to know is how you are feeling inside you to the words that are coming out to be outside of you.
>
> Do you always have the same kind of feeling in relation to the sounds as the words come out of you or do you not. All this has so much to do with grammar and with poetry and with prose.
>
> Words have to do everything in poetry and prose and some writers write more in articles and prepositions and some say you should write in nouns, and of course one has to think of everything.
>
> A noun is a name of anything, why after a thing is named write about it. A name is adequate or it is not. If it is adequate then why go on calling it, if it is not then calling it by its name does no good.
>
> GERTRUDE STEIN, "Poetry and Grammar"

If we lived in a world where all of us were intent only on "making language mean," it would be a strange, obsessed world indeed. Such one-sidedness needs balancing, and the best balance can be expressed by the phrase, "letting language play."

How does one develop this sense of language as play? The fact is, for most adults, it involves recapturing a long-lost skill from childhood. If you can observe a child's use of language you may recall your own first exhilarating experiences with words. The child uses language almost as though it had physicality—tries out words, tests phrases, sings some syllables until a meaning emerges, tosses a basketful of words in the air and watches as they float and glide.

> I've had my supper,
>   And had my supper,
>   And HAD my supper and all;
> I've heard the story
>   Of Cinderella,
>   And how she went to the ball;
> I've cleaned my teeth,
>   And I've said my prayers,
>   And I've cleaned and said them right;
> And they've all of them been
>   And kissed me lots,
>   They've all of them said "Good-
>   night."
>
> So—here I am in the dark alone
>   There's nobody here to see;
>   I think to myself,
>   I play to myself,
>   And nobody knows what I say to
>   myself;
> Here I am in the dark alone,
>   What is it going to be?
> I can think whatever I like to think,
> I can play whatever I like to play,
> I can laugh whatever I like to laugh,
>   There's nobody here but me.
>
> I'm talking to a rabbit . . .
>   I'm talking to the sun . . .
> I think I am a hundred—
>   I'm one.
> I'm lying in a forest . . .
>   I'm lying in a cave . . .
> I'm talking to a Dragon . . .
>   I'm BRAVE
> I'm lying on my left side . . .
>   I'm lying on my right . . .

                    I'll play a lot tomorrow . . .
                    . . . .
                    I'll think a lot tomorrow . . .
                    . . . .
                    I'll laugh . . .
                                    a lot. . . .
                                    tomorrow . . .
                    (Heigh-ho!)
                    Goodnight.
        A. A. MILNE, "In the Dark," *Now We Are Six*

Perhaps we can capture something of the child's delight in
language even if we are too self-conscious to start babbling. Just
to see what might come out we can in effect babble on paper. Put
a pencil to paper and start writing whatever the pencil wants to
write:

contact . . . relieve . . . blue . . . laugh . . . gum . . . sum . . .
bum . . . glum . . . tum . . . tummy . . . dummy . . . gummy . . .
rummy . . . gloomy . . . boomy . . . roomy . . . the rummy bum . . .
the boomy glum . . . the dummy laugh . . . the sunny gaff . . . the
boomy voice . . . the tummy glummy . . . the gummy tummy . . .
the rummy tummy is gloomy with booms . . . the dummy rummy
is boomy with glooms . . . the rat and the cat are fat with splat . . .
the ant and the fly are speckled with rye. . . .

Babbling on paper might lead to something, or it might not.
If a word or phrase catches hold in the mind, it might cling there
until it becomes surrounded with a number of chattering com-
panions, vibrating to each other and creating new syllables, new
words, new phrases, new ideas—and maybe new insights into
the resonance of language, the distances it can travel on its own.

            Besides the nouns and the adjectives
            there are verbs and adverbs. Verbs
            and adverbs are more interesting. In
            the first place they have one very
            nice quality and that is that they can
            be so mistaken. It is wonderful the
            number of mistakes a verb can make and
            that is equally true of its adverb.
            Nouns and adjectives never can make
            mistakes can never be mistaken but
            verbs can be so endlessly, both as to

> what they do and how they agree or
> disagree with whatever they do. The
> same is true of adverbs.
>
> GERTRUDE STEIN, "Poetry and Grammar"

In attempting to let language play, we are merely renewing an attitude, a feeling, a freedom we all once had with language in our earlier years.

Engine, engine, number nine,
Running on Chicago line.
If it's polished, it will shine.
Engine, engine, number nine.

Or:

Knife and fork!
Bottle and cork!
That's the way to
Spell New York!

B. A. BOTKIN
A Treasure of American Folklore

These or similar verses we once recited or chanted in our games, letting language play as we ourselves play. A bit later, we all probably went through a phase when we collected and passed on such limericks as:

A cheerful old bear at the zoo
Could always find something to do;
    When it bored him, you know,
    To walk to and fro,
He reversed it, and walked fro and to.

Or:

A father once said to his son,
"The next time you make up a pun,
    Go out in the yard,
    And kick yourself hard,
And I shall begin when you've done."

EVAN ESAR, *Humorous English*

Puns. Ah, yes. Who has not punned, at one time or another, sometimes without thinking. " 'Pun my word, what is that I see on the page but a pun! Around and around the world, the pun never sets on the ubiquitous punster. Even when told, 'Go and pun no more,' the hooked punster cannot kick his pundit. Forgive us our puns, as we forgive those who pun against us."

An early nineteenth-century poet, Thomas Hood, wrote:

Tim Turpin he was gravel blind,
    And ne'er had seen the skies:
For Nature, when his head was made,
    Forgot to dot his eyes.

So, like Christmas pedagogue,
    Poor Tim was forc'd to do—
Look out for pupils, for he had
    A vacancy for two.

There's some have specs to help their sight
    Of objects dim and small:
But Tim had *specks* within his eyes,
    And could not see at all.
        THOMAS HOOD, *Selected Poems*

There are nineteen more stanzas for those interested in poor Tim's sad fate—and the puns continue to pop all over the place.

Sometimes the oversolemnity of language use invites a playful reply, a parody that makes fun of the original. Edgar Allan Poe wrote a poem about a young man grieving for the loss of his girl. Here is the first stanza of "The Raven":

Once upon a midnight dreary, while I pondered, weak and weary,
Over many a quaint and curious volume of forgotten lore,
While I nodded, nearly napping, suddenly there came a tapping,
As of some one gently rapping, rapping at my chamber door.
" 'Tis some visitor," I muttered, "tapping at my chamber door—
        Only this and nothing more."

In "Ravin's of Piute Poet Poe," C. L. Edson presents a similar situation in rhythms strikingly—jarringly—familiar:

Once up a midnight dreary, eerie, scary,
I was wary, I was weary, full of worry, thinking of my lost Lenore,
Of my cheery, airy, faery, fiery Dearie—(Nothing more).
I was napping, when a tapping on the overlapping coping, woke me
    grapping, yapping, groping . . . toward the rapping. I went hopping,
    leaping . . . hoping that the rapping on the coping
Was my little lost Lenore.
That on opening the shutter to admit the latter critter, in she'd
    flutter from the gutter with her bitter eyes a-glitter;

So I opened wide the door, what was there? The dark weir and the
  drear moor,—or I'm a liar—the dark mire, the drear moor,
  the mere door and nothing more!

Then in stepped a stately raven, shaven like the bard of Avon;
  yes, a-rovin' grievin' Raven, seeking haven at my door.
Yes, that shaven, rovin' Raven had been movin' (Get me Stephen)
  for the warm and lovin' haven of my stove an' oven door—
Oven door and nothing more.

These tongue-twisting lines run on for three or four more stanzas,
growing increasingly absurd (and fun) as they run. Poe's poem
should be read aloud to enjoy the intensity of its melancholy; and
the Edson parody must be read aloud to savor the wickedness of
its wit and the sharpness of its thrust.

Beside that there are conjunctions,
and a conjunction is not varied but
it has a force that need not make any
one feel that they are dull. Conjunctions have made themselves live
by their work. They work and as they
work they live and even when they do
not work and in these days they do
not always live by work still nevertheless they do live.
  GERTRUDE STEIN, "Poetry and Grammar"

Language play can be serious as well as fun. Indeed, when
the playfulness is used to support some serious purpose, it often
heightens the meaning. Observe, for example, the following poem
by William Shakespeare in which stale and predictable language
is turned against itself to satirize outmoded traditions and hypo-
critical attitudes:

My Mistress' eyes are nothing like the sun,
Coral is far more red than her lips' red.
If snow be white, why then her breasts are dun,
If hairs be wires, black wires grow on her head.
I have seen roses damasked, red and white,
But no such roses see I in her cheeks.
And in some perfumes is there more delight
Than in the breath that from my mistress reeks.
I love to hear her speak, yet well I know

That music hath a far more pleasing sound.
I grant I never saw a goddess go,
My mistress, when she walks, treads on the ground.
    And yet, by Heaven, I think my love as rare
    As any she belied with false compare.
           WILLIAM SHAKESPEARE, "Sonnet 130"

Letting language play is another way of limbering up the imagination, or opening it up to the undertones and overtones, the subtlety and resonance, the tricks and surprises when words get together to let meaning happen. Sometimes the nonsense works its way to a kind of sense, a deeper sense than we might at first have guessed. Language let out to play might bring back treasures little suspected. Language given its freedom can surprise us into truth.

> Very fine is my valentine.
> Very fine and very mine.
> Very mine is my valentine very mine
>   and very fine.
> Very fine is my valentine and mine,
>   very fine very mine and mine is my
>   valentine.
>   GERTRUDE STEIN, "A Very Valentine"

DISCUSSION

Recall the limericks or other short poems that you hear in your daily experience. Comment on the playful use of language in them.

Collect or create a batch a riddles and test them out on others in your group.

How many playful nursery rhymes can you resurrect in your memory from childhood? Why did these poems stick with you?

Create a collection of puns. Build one pun on another. Frolic.
Here is a beginning:

Every individual goes through a crisis when he reaches the age of punburty.
To pun or not to pun, that is the question.
Please don't pun me to a wall.

IDEAS AND EXPERIMENTS

There is really only one assignment for this chapter: Play with
language. And enjoy it. Get a stack of blank paper and turn
your language loose. Indulge in some linguistic doodling. Drift
from one word to another. Link words when you are moved
to; develop phrases when you feel like it. Free associate from
word to word, image to image, idea to idea. Write a joke. Write
a riddle. Write a limerick or satire. Write some sheer and
utter nonsense. Turn your pun to penning.

FURTHER POINTS OF DEPARTURE

Gather some books written especially for young children and examine the appeal of language play which they have.

Write some playful children's stories or verses yourself.

Alice goes to "A Mad Tea-Party":

"Your hair wants cutting," said the Hatter. He had been looking at
Alice for some time with great curiosity, and this was his first
speech.

"You should learn not to make personal remarks," Alice said with
some severity: "it's very rude."

The Hatter opened his eyes very wide on hearing this; but all he *said*
was "Why is a raven like a writing-desk?"

"Come, we shall have some fun now!" thought Alice. "I'm glad
they've begun asking riddles—I believe I can guess that," she
added aloud.

"Do you mean that you think you can find out the answer to it?" said
the March Hare.

"Exactly so," said Alice.

"Then you should say what you mean," the March Hare went on.

"I do," Alice hastily replied; "at least—at least I mean what I say—
that's the same thing, you know."

"Not the same thing a bit!" said the Hatter. "Why, you might just as
well say that 'I see what I eat' is the same thing as 'I eat what
I see'!"

"You might just as well say," added the March Hare, "that 'I like
what I get' is the same thing as 'I get what I like'!"

"You might just as well say," added the Dormouse, which seemed to be
talking in its sleep, "that 'I breathe when I sleep' is the same thing
as 'I sleep when I breathe.' "

"It *is* the same thing with you," said the Hatter, and here the
conversation dropped, and the party sat silent for a minute, while
Alice thought over all she could remember about ravens and
writing-desks, which wasn't much.

LEWIS CARROLL, Alice in Wonderland

Show the ways that Lewis Carroll is letting language play
here. Discuss the possible serious meanings intended in the
passage.

"Why is a raven like a writing-desk?" Does this riddle have an answer? Carroll gave one: "because it can produce a few notes,
although they are very flat, and it is never put the wrong end
front." How satisfactory is the answer?

Find other passages in the Alice books that seem to let language
play? Comment on their playfulness and their seriousness.

14

Language and community

. . . while [language] may be looked
upon as a symbolic system which
reports or refers to or otherwise
substitutes for direct experience, it
does not as a matter of actual behavior stand apart from or run
parallel to direct experience but
completely interpenetrates with it.

It is this constant interplay between
language and experience which removes
language from the cold status of such
purely and simply symbolic systems as
mathematical symbolism or flag signal-
ing. This interpenetration is not
only an intimate associative fact; it
is also a contextual one. It is
important to realize that language
may not only refer to experience or
even mold, interpret, and discover
experience, but that it also substitutes for it in the sense that in
those sequences of interpersonal
behavior which form the greater part
of our daily lives speech and action
supplement each other and do each
other's work in a web of unbroken
pattern.

EDWARD SAPIR, *Language*

As language flows within the self, helping to define and delimit the interior world of the self, so it also flows from the inside
to the world around and beyond the self, helping to define and

delimit and delineate that world—a world made up (as in the old definition of a *noun*) of persons, places, things. Language plays a primary role in connecting us with the persons, places, and things of the universe.

Probably the most vital role of language is its serving as the basis for the interrelationship of all human beings. We admire and we ridicule, we hate and we love—in language. Moreover, language serves as the substance of the web that holds together social groups, small and large, national and international. But language is much more than merely communicative—it is creative. We create ourselves, our relationships, our friends and enemies, our neighbors and acquaintances through language.

> Through the Thou a man becomes I.
> That which confronts him comes and
> disappears, relational events condense,
> then are scattered, and in the change
> consciousness of the unchanging part-
> ner, of the I, grows clear, and each
> time stronger. To be sure, it is
> still seen caught in the web of the
> relation of the Thou, as the increas-
> ingly distinguishable feature of that
> which reaches out to and yet is not
> the Thou. But it continually breaks
> through with more power, till a time
> comes when it bursts its bonds, and
> the I confronts itself for a moment,
> separated as though it were a Thou;
> as quickly to take possession of
> itself and from then on to enter into
> relations in consciousness of itself."
> MARTIN BUBER, *I and Thou*

Thus we are deeply concerned about our public use of language, for it forms our vital connection with the outside world. If we have not made ourselves clear, we try again. Or we go over and over again in our minds a crucial event in our lives, thinking what we could have said, might have said, tried to say. What we do, in effect, is to evaluate our linguistic identification, reconsidering our self-portrait in language, while forming an increasingly complex set of links with the language community.

Although there is much that we can control personally in our language use, there is much that is beyond our control because of the language communities to which we belong. *Communities* must be used here in the plural, because all of us belong to a set of communities that determine in part aspects of our language.

We speak English, but we do not say "Zounds, methinks I hear alarums. Fie on't." That is, we are not Elizabethans and do not speak like a character from a Shakespearean play. Indeed not. No one can decide in which century, decade or year he or she will be born. Any person living in the twentieth century will assimilate an English that is quite distinct from Elizabethan English, although it inherits much vitality from it. Those of us who speak and use English today are, by necessity, speakers and users of the English language as it has evolved up to this point in history, and this language is different not only from that of the Elizabethan period but also from that of one hundred or even ten years ago. It is an observed fact (not only of English but of all known tongues) that language changes continuously. The only static language is a dead language—a language no longer used by living people.

These statements appear so obvious that perhaps they do not need saying, but the facts that flow from these truisms are some of the most misunderstood in our culture: We speak the American dialect we speak because of the region of the country in which we are born and live; and we speak the variety of that dialect because of the social class in which we have been nurtured.

> But [in] . . . history, region, and society—[a speaker] is more or less caught up in forces beyond his control. No man can change the generation or place of his birth; his attempts to change the social variety of his speech will be determined by the kind of education he receives and the kind of person he associates with, and opportunities to make a drastic change are not as common as we would like.
>
> RAVEN I. MC DAVID, JR.
> "Historical, Regional and Social Variation"

We all speak English, but we speak it with differences, which are sometimes very noticeable. The differences may be in pronunciation, in vocabulary, in sentence pattern, or in other elements. With them arise problems and misunderstandings.

It is not unusual for members of a community to find anyone who does not conform to its characteristics an object of ridicule or contempt, as inferior—or, at the least, incorrect. This reaction to difference is probably rooted in fear and is a universal human trait. Most of us have experienced such fears, and now remember how they were modified by knowledge or education.

> There is not in language (or in any other form of human behavior) a simple opposition between good and bad, but a complicated set of interrelated variations; it is necessary for linguists themselves to sort out the many dimensions in which usage may vary and show how these variations are related to each other.
>
> RAVEN I. MC DAVID, JR.
> "Historical, Regional and Social Variation"

By now most people are attuned to the differences in pronunciation of New Englanders, Southerners, Southwesterners, Westerners, and others. But we still encounter accusations that this or that speech is wrong, merely because it is different. A person may say "idear," or "Y'all come, heah?" or "He be goin'," or "Where is the warsh rag?" or "It's a fur piece down the road." Such differences in the language are signs not of impoverishment but of riches. Variety, as someone has observed, is the spice of life. Dialect difference can be the spice of language.

> American educational institutions is continuing they role as passive reflectors of a racist, inhumane society. In part, the contemporary madness bees manifest in the "language deprivation" teaching strategies for the "disadvantaged" Black American. Suddenly!!!!! after more than three centuries on this continent, the educational and societal consensus is that Blacks have a "language problem." But wasn't nobody complainin bout Black speech in 1619 when the first

cargo of Africans was brought here
on the Good Ship Jesus—yeah, that's
right. Nor in 1719, 1819, 1919—
really, it wasn't till bout the 1950's
when it became evident that Afros was
really beginning to make some economic
headway in America that everybody and
they momma started talkin bout we
didn talk right. (It was bout that
time—1956 to be exact—that yours
truly was a college freshman forced
to enroll in speech therapy—un-huh,
you heard me—cause of my "regional"—
now they just say "Black"—dialect.)
                          GENEVA SMITHERMAN, "Soul 'N Style"

The dialect we find ourselves using, because of the accidents
of the time and place of our births, is as good—as functional—as
any other dialect of the language. It can perform as simply or
complexly as we want it to, and it can enable us to lead lives as
enriched by language as possible. Moreover, it is a valuable part
of our heritage and identification, and to give it up would be almost the same as denying a part of the self.

. . . I would emphasize the incor-
rectness and fallaciousness of the
apparently widespread belief that
speaking a nonstandard dialect is
somehow a sign of a deficiency in
thought or in mental development.
There may be some connection between
language and thought, but it is not
exhibited in nonstandard speech. Our
children who are speakers of nonstandard dialects—whether they be
blacks, Puerto Ricans, or Chicanos,
are not the victims of undeveloped
language codes. Their languages have
principles and rules similar to those
that govern any language.
                          JOHN B. CARROLL, "Language and Cognition"

As for our writing: The more aware we are of our own dialect
and the dialects of other areas, the more resources we have to

draw on when we put pen to paper. Each dialect develops colorful expressions and ways of saying things. Think of such disparate individuals as Abraham Lincoln, Eleanor Roosevelt, Nikita Khrushchev, Margaret Mead, Marie Curie, or John F. Kennedy. All of these people were, in some sense, people of the world, but they had their roots deeply embedded in particular places, particular times—and they were nourished linguistically by the dialects into which they were born. Much of their identity derived from the individuality, the richness of the language of the geographical region and social level where they found themselves at birth.

As for them, so for us. We should always cherish the language of the community of our origin, however far we travel, physically or mentally, from that community, however many other languages or dialects we acquire and use. To forget or suppress one dialect as we acquire another is to lose a part of the self. To add another dialect to the basic one we have is to extend our linguistic resources and deepen the possibilities of self.

Even so, we want to put this discussion into the context of "writing in reality," for it would be naive of textwriters or students or teachers to ignore the demands for correctness that are imposed upon a writer by audiences, or to argue that one should cherish his or her natural dialect to the exclusion of all concern for correctness. Perhaps the most helpful thing we can do is help to destroy some myths about standard English, or good English, that have circulated freely:

Standard English is not a "pure" form of the language or language as "it was meant to be." (It is, in fact, little more than a dialect which—through historical accident—has risen to cultural dominance.)

It is not a magic key to employment, success in school, or a happy marriage. (While many claim you must possess standard English to succeed in life, evidence to the contrary abounds.)

It is not fixed in its form. (Like all dialects, standard English changes.)

It is not consistent from one area of the country to another. (As *Webster's* notes, in some parts of the country, "ain't" is commonly accepted in conversations.)

It is not spoken only by the "best" people in the country. (Nor does speaking standard English make a "bad" person "good.")

It is not learned through the study of grammar. (Dialects are learned through day-to-day use, not the study of rules and laws.)

Defining standard English is difficult; in fact, a good many linguists refuse to use the term at all, arguing that there are too many different forms and varieties of "standard" for the word to have any meaning. Robert Pooley has suggested that good English is "that form of speech which is appropriate to the purposes of the speaker, true to the language as it is, and comfortable to the speaker and listener,"[1] and that definition can serve the writer very usefully.

It is also useful to talk of a kind of standard English (SE) that has been variously labeled schoolroom standard or media standard or publication standard. This book is written in it; so is *Time* magazine. It is the English used on the nightly news and spoken (for the most part) in the halls of Congress. Having been drilled in it from about sixth grade on, you are probably familiar with most of its features already; it involves distinctions between such words and phrases as:

> *lay—lie*
> *sit—set*
> *He is going—He be going*
> *He has gone—He done gone*

and, of course:

> *I haven't—I ain't*

Whether one chooses to use SE some or all of the time is an individual decision and should, as Pooley implies, depend on the situation. There are times when using SE is important—or more accurately, when failure to use it has negative consequences (for instance, most college examinations or job applications should be written in SE). There are other times when SE doesn't matter much—talking with friends, writing rough drafts, or writing for personal pleasure. The writer needs to assess whether or not the use of SE is important and required for the situation.

Correctness, then, is something that the writer needs to consider, but he or she needs to keep the concern for correctness in perspective. In all human relationships, language is crucial and creative, but the correctness (or good grammar) has little to do

---

[1] Robert Pooley, *Teaching English Usage,* National Council of Teachers of English, 1964, p. 14.

with language's creative role in these relationships. Creativity is sustained not by language that is correct or proper but rather by language that is in some sense genuine.

Walt Whitman's poem "A Noiseless Patient Spider" may be read symbolically as a poem about human relationships which are initiated and sustained by the launched "filaments" of language, whether comprised of words, gestures, or both.

A noiseless patient spider,
I mark'd where on a little promontory it stood isolated,
Mark'd how to explore the vacant vast surrounding.

It launch'd forth filament, filament, filament, out of itself,
Ever unreeling them, ever tirelessly speeding them.

And you O my soul where you stand,
Surrounded, detached, in measureless oceans of space,
Ceaselessly musing, venturing, throwing, seeking, the spheres
    to connect them,
Till the bridge you will need be form'd, till the ductile anchor hold,
Till the gossamer thread you fling catch somewhere, O my soul.

"Ceaselessly musing, venturing, throwing" we live our lives, spinning out the web of our existence through the community of language.

DISCUSSION

Consider:

A riot is the language of the unheard.
MARTIN LUTHER KING

In the essay "Soul 'N Style," which was cited earlier, Dr. Geneva Smitherman (who writes for publication in a version of her own Black dialect) sketches out three dominant views of dialects and schooling:

Eradicationist—argues that all nonstandard dialects should be expunged from the schools.

Bidialectalist—feels that there is nothing wrong with a non-standard dialect, but that all children should learn standard English in addition.

Legitimizer—believes that dialect differences do not interfere significantly with communication, and all dialects should be considered standard.

Which position do you hold? Why?

Do dialects make a difference? How do you react to people whose dialect differs from your own? Have you ever felt self-conscious about your own dialect? Why?

IDEAS AND EXPERIMENTS

Examine the dialect you speak, and write an account of its characteristics compared with one from a different region.

Find someone from another region and collaborate on a list or dictionary of the differences between your two dialects.

Experiment with writing in a dialect other than your own. What are the problems you encounter?

Deliberately use some nonstandard expressions in standard situations. Say: "ain't"; "don't gonna go"; or "I sez to my friend." What happens? Explore the biases others have toward speakers of nonstandard English.

FURTHER POINTS OF DEPARTURE

Examine and write an essay on the dialect you find in a work of literature. Some possible works to explore: Mark Twain, *Huckleberry Finn;* J. D. Salinger, *Catcher in the Rye;* Flannery O'Connor, *Wise Blood;* James Baldwin, *Go Tell it on the Mountain;* Piri Thomas, *Down These Mean Streets.* Don't forget the poets: Allen Ginsberg, Amiri Baraka, Gwendolyn Brooks.

Conduct interviews with friends, strangers, classmates, relatives, associates, and attempt to assess how people feel about those who talk "different." How accurate are people's assessment of the relationship between language and community?

15

Language, society, and morality

Most people who bother with the matter
at all would admit that the English
language is in a bad way, but it is
generally assumed that we cannot by
conscious action do anything about it.
Our civilization is decadent, and our
language—so the argument runs—must
inevitably share in the general col-
lapse. It follows that any struggle
against the abuse of language is
sentimental archaism, like preferring
candles to electric light or hansom
cabs to aeroplanes. Underneath this
lies the half-conscious belief that
language is a natural growth and not
an instrument which we shape for our
own purpose. . . . [The English lan-
guage] becomes ugly and inaccurate
because our thoughts are foolish, but
the slovenliness of our language makes
it easier for us to have foolish
thoughts. The point is the process
is reversible.
GEORGE ORWELL, "Politics and the English Language"

From the last and highest promontory
of time, we may see that the truth is
not made up of words at all, only that
we have had to use words to lure it
from its hiding places. And after all
is said, it may be (if we can know

what this means) that the truth is not
more than being itself, innocent,
eternal being. But here and now we
are obliged to use language and human
thought with which to draw up our
agreement with reality. Truth is the
name we give to the highest and deepest
insights, the fruit of long experience, to those ideas and phenomena
which have stood the test of our
straining at them, which we have
judged most likely to endure, which
are universally human, and about which
disagreement is only inconsequential
quibbling. Unfortunately, the wish
for power is sometimes greater than
the wish for truth. People sometimes
invent the "truth" where it suits
them to do so. And sometimes the
"truth" seems to be whatever strong
and powerful men say it is, and we
are stampeded into thinking something
is true that deep within us we know
is not.

WELLER EMBLER, "Language and Truth"

Perhaps no issue has been of greater concern to writers and
to those who are interested in understanding the writing process
than the relationship between language and morality. As we have
suggested, language is intricately connected with the creation of
self; we use language to construct a view of reality ("truth," to
use Weller Embler's phrase) and to share our view of the truth
with others. As both Orwell and Embler imply in the epigraphs
that open this chapter, language is not always used skillfully,
wisely, or ethically in this process. Many people are word-bound.
Trapped into accepting words at literal or face value, they fail
to recognize that all language is an abstraction—a process of
symbolization—that words represent a person's approach to the
truth, not the truth itself. Semanticist Alfred Korzybski pointed
out that too many people treat words as if they were objects and
act as if abstractions and concepts were real things, with the result that their thinking and communication are limited, their
imagination constrained.

So many people are trapped in this way that it has always

been a temptation for the strong and articulate to use language as a way of imposing their own truths or reality on others, using language to shape the "real" world to their own liking.

> Except for the fact that we sometimes act without thinking, it would seem obvious that how we act is determined by how we think. But even when we act without thinking, our actions are likely to follow the lines laid down by our patterns of thought, which in turn are determined by the language we use. The intellectually naive often objectify language as if it were something "out there"; to be examined independently of speakers or hearers. But language, to be language, has meaning, and meanings are not "out there." Meanings are semantic reactions that take place <u>in people.</u> A language is therefore not just the sounds and the spellings, but more importantly, the whole repertory of semantic reactions which sounds and spellings produce in those who understand the language.
>
> s. i. HAYAKAWA, *The Use and Abuse of Language*

When speakers or writers recognize that meaning resides in people, not in the words themselves, they can, if they wish, use words deliberately to create set reactions in their readers or listeners. Shout: "Tyranny!" "Infamy!" "Motherhood!" "Freedom!" or "Honesty!" from the lecture platform and you will trigger a more or less common set of responses in your audience. If you use euphemism, vague language, irrational but dramatic appeals, you can—all too frequently—control the reactions and thoughts of listeners very deftly.

Of course, the problem of the misuse of language did not originate in our own time. In classical Greece, declamation was a highly prized skill, and the person who could move the masses through oratory became an important political figure, which placed a premium on the golden tongued orator who could make "the worse appear the better cause." In *The Republic,* Plato banned rhetoricians from his ideal society, arguing that public speakers were mere hucksters with no insight into the ideals of truth. In his society, their functions would be taken over by philosopher-statesmen, who were concerned solely with the truth and therefore were in no need of rhetorical artifice or trickery. Aristotle was a bit more realistic about the difficulties of finding elusive truth. He recognized that given the nature of human beings and society, some nonlogical use of language was inevitable, and that invariably people would misuse language to some degree, drawing on rhetorical devices—the rhetoric of propaganda—to sway the minds of the audience. Aristotle's solution was to urge wider education in rhetoric for all people (or at least, for Greek young men) on the argument that given two orators of equal knowledge and skill in rhetoric, the truth or better cause would invariably win out. (This confidence in the inherent obviousness of truth may seem a touch idealistic, but certainly his suggestion that the young be educated in the principles of rhetoric was sound.)

In our own time, of course, the question of ethics and language persists, heightened by the proliferation of media communications. Aristotle and Plato needed to concern themselves with ethics and language principally in oratory; the twentieth-century person must be concerned about the use of language in newspapers and magazines, advertising and propaganda, television, radio, literature, and film. Instant communication increases not only our vision but also our vulnerability. Further, in the twentieth century, the skill of media users has dramatically increased through careful study and research. Aristotle noted that an orator could effectively disarm an opponent's argument by tactfully shifting the topic to other areas or by including a distracting but irrelevant argument, but Aristotle never saw that done with the sophistication of a contemporary television commercial for beer, laundry powder, or mouthwash.

In the twentieth century, persuasive techniques have also gone underground. Drawing on some of the basic theories of psychology, those who would persuade us use techniques aimed directly at our subconscious minds, bypassing the natural barriers created by rational, skeptical thought. We have even witnessed experiments in so-called subliminal persuasion, bombarding the consumer with messages that he or she never sees.

The dangers in this bombardment by language are, for the most part, apparent. Our century has seen Adolph Hitler rise to power using conventional rhetorical techniques to enflame and captivate an entire nation, culminating in the horrors of World War II. We have watched American involvement in a brush-fire war in Southeast Asia grow to astounding proportions, all masked beneath subtle, but reassuring euphemisms from military and political leaders. We have seen television advertising grow into a billion-dollar industry, and we have observed politicians adopting the techniques of the television commercial.

There is an even greater danger than the overt manipulation which can take place when language is misused—deliberately, or otherwise—and that is the loss of identity which results when an individual or society succumbs to the misuse of language.

In *1984*, George Orwell probed some of the possibilities of a society in which thought-control techniques have been applied to an entire population. As an administrator explained to Winston Smith, one of the few remaining free people in the novel, succumbing to the thought control of "the Party" is an act of self-destruction:"

When you delude yourself into thinking that you see something, you assume that everyone else sees the same thing as you. But I tell you, Winston, that reality is not external. Reality exists in the human mind, nowhere else. Not in the individual mind, which can make mistakes, and in any case soon perishes; only in the mind of the Party, which is collective and immortal. Whatever the Party holds to be truth *is* truth. It is impossible to see reality except by looking through the eyes of the Party. That is the fact that you have got to relearn, Winston. It needs an act of self-destruction, an effort of the will.

Whenever one is controlled in this way—be it "falling for" the image of a political candidate rather than his substance, buying a pack of cigarettes because the advertising rhetoric pledges "a breath of springtime," failing to see through a jaded or biased news story, taking a euphemistic government pronouncement at face value—a bit of the self is eroded and lost, the self that we so carefully build up from childhood. If this happens to an entire society, an entire people can lose their identity, becoming the self-destructive force that Germany was in the thirties and forties, or, perhaps, the plastic society which some allege the United States has become.

What, if anything, can be done to preserve one's self, especially given the wave of language that inundates us in an electronic society? No easy answers are forthcoming. One can choose to wait for the arrival of Plato's ideal society of logic and reason, but practical logic calls for recognition of Aristotle's real world where the logical and illogical, the ethical and immoral uses of language, are mixed.

One solution, implied by Aristotle, is increased awareness of language and the ways in which it functions. People are more vulnerable to psychological appeal, to euphemism, and to propaganda when they are unaware of its existence and effects. Once you know and can identify the techniques being used, they lose much of their effectiveness. Thus a consciousness of language and how it functions in society is an important first step toward controlling the use and misuse of language.

A vastly more important (and far less tangible) solution centers on one's perception of self and the strength and confidence with which one holds to that self. In Orwell's *1984*, Winston Smith rebels and almost survives the onslaught of propaganda from "the Party" and "Big Brother" because his sense of self and reality is indomitable. While others around him meekly accept the "doublethink" thrown at them by the Party, Winston steadfastly maintains his sense of reality—he *knows* the truth, and therefore, artful strategies do not work on him.

As Winston demonstrated, it takes enormous courage at times to keep one's identity intact, to resist the appeals of media, to avoid succumbing to the attempts of others to shape one's world view to their image. But once one has achieved a sense of self— through reading, writing, experiencing, growing—the defenses are high. The solution to the problem of morality and language, lies not in language, but in the selves who use, shape, and are shaped by language.

DISCUSSION

Is it immoral to make "the worse appear the better cause"? Are politicians acting unethically when they use propaganda and advertising techniques to sell themselves? Is it legitimate for a public speaker to bend his description of the facts in order to persuade? Discuss the moral and immoral uses of language in society. Can you come up with a "Code of Ethics" for the use and misuse of language?

Marshall McLuhan has remarked that the "medium is the message," and advertisers and propagandists agree and act on the idea. Make a comparative study of two media, say television and radio, or newspapers and magazines. What are the possibilities for the use and misuse of language in each?

George Orwell claimed in 1946 that the misuse of language was
    reversible. Living more than thirty years later, do you agree?

Nominate the ten worst commercials currently blasting their way
    into your life via TV.

Do you agree with those who argue that television has turned us
    into "a plastic society"?

IDEAS AND EXPERIMENTS

One of the best ways to build defenses against the use and misuse
    of language is to understand how it is used for persuasive
    purposes. Explore the forms of persuasion. Working with
    several other people, choose a controversial topic, issue, or
    idea—pollution, youth and age, urban decay, political reform
    —and develop as much persuasive material as you can to
    push your cause or commitment with an audience. Con-
    sider writing essaylike materials—editorials, speeches, mono-
    graphs—as well as advertising-oriented ones—bumper stick-
    ers, television commercials, newspaper ads. In what ways can
    both kinds of materials be used ethically and unethically to
    promote a cause?

Wallow in euphemism, gobbledeygook, and bureaucratic prose.
    Choose a message and mask it under layers of misleading and
    vague prose. In doing so, you will come to understand more
    fully how euphemism can be used against you.

Invent a new common household product and write a satirical
    television commercial for it.

Write an All-American Fourth of July speech on behalf of a can-
    didate who has little substance but considerable charm, who
    gains election through image projection rather than real
    issues. Talk over the rhetoric of politics after this experiment.

Choose an issue of current interest and importance; argue both
    sides of it in separate essays, being as persuasive as you can
    in each. What happens to your self when you are arguing the
    side you do not especially believe?

FURTHER POINTS OF DEPARTURE

In *Language and Thought in Action* (Harcourt Brace Jovanovich,
    1972), S. I. Hayakawa observed that popular songs frequently
    involve the abuse of language by creating false or stereotyped

visions of life and love. Examine the lyrics of several current songs to assess the validity of his charge. What, if any, influence might lyrics have on shaping our national self-image?

Read Hayakawa's book, which is concerned with the process of "meaning-making" and the use and misuse of language, and prepare a set of notes or observations on "language and thought in action."

"Newspeak" is a political language used in Orwell's *1984;* its functions and roles are explained in an appendix to the book. Read Orwell's description and consider the accuracy and validity of his assertion about language and thought.

Read, enjoy, and report on Ivan C. Petersen's *The Great American Blow-up: Puffery in American Advertising* (Wisconsin, 1975).

16

The language and impact of media

THE CITY no longer exists, except as a cultural ghost for tourists. Any highway eatery with its TV set, newspaper, and magazine is as cosmopolitan as New York or Paris.

The METROPOLIS today is a classroom; the ads are its teachers. The classroom is an obsolete detention home, a feudal dungeon.

The metropolis is OBSOLETE.

Ask the Army

The handwriting is on the celluloid walls of Hollywood; the Age of Writing has passed. We must invent a NEW METAPHOR, restructure our thoughts and feelings. The new media are not bridges between man and nature; they are nature.

Gutenberg made all history SIMULTANE-OUS: the transportable book brought the world of the dead into the space of the gentleman's library; the telegraph brought the entire world of the living to the workman's breakfast table.

NOBODY yet knows the language inherent in the new technological culture; we

are all deaf-blind mutes in terms of
the new situation. Our most impres-
sive words and thoughts betray us by
referring to the previously existent,
not to the present.

WE ARE BACK IN ACOUSTIC SPACE

We begin again to structure the primor-
dial feelings and emotions from which
3000 years of literacy divorced us.
                    MARSHALL MCLUHAN, *Counterblast*

Motion pictures, the phonograph, radio, and television all
have radically changed the way we live and the way we encounter the world. The movies deeply affected the theater, effectively
killing the popular stage and leaving only a legitimate theater
that is constantly struggling for survival. The phonograph, which
made it possible to preserve musical performance and speech for
an indefinite period, brought into the home sounds and words that
previously could be heard only in large auditoriums with large
audiences. The radio brought a culture of its own, constructed
entirely on sound and consisting of home-delivered music, drama,
news coverage, political speeches, and much more. And when
television added picture to sound, electronic technology had made
it possible, as never before, to bring the entire world into the home.

The marvels of these media are such as to confound the
imagination, especially when it is realized that new developments
will undoubtedly refine, extend, and improve these media. As we
drive across the country, noting the ubiquity of the TV antenna,
we are shocked into an awareness of how much the nation is held
in conformity by this medium. When we see that people in New

York and California laugh at the same jokes at the same time of day, that they hear the same political speeches, and that they see the same news items of the most recent disaster, it becomes clear that the country has become homogeneous. We have a common culture as never before in history—this in spite of the fact that there are many more people spread out over greater geographical areas than ever before. It has, indeed, become possible for the first time in history for the world to become "one world"—technologically possible, that is.

Marvels exist beyond the unity made possible by the mass media. Among the most important must be placed the journalistic possibilities. News from all over the world may be brought instantly into our homes, informing an entire people—on occasion an entire world—of events that may be occurring in some obscure, remote spot. Within the past decade, public response to the Viet Nam war gives evidence of the enormous impact "instant" coverage of news events has on a people. The events, moreover, may be given a visual presentation that does much more than inform—it can add a dimension of reality that evokes deep emotional response: tears at a natural disaster, fear at a criminal bombing, outrage at brutality. In addition to news, discussion programs—presenting prominent people, politicians, professors, and just plain people—may examine important public and political issues of the day, informing, provoking thought, developing interest and awareness. In addition to the journalistic possibilities are the marvelous imaginative and dramatic possibilities. In our time, more people have witnessed a Shakespearean play (thanks to TV) than ever before in history. There have been original TV dramas and other programs of considerable merit—poetry readings, ballets, concerts by symphonic orchestras, reruns of classic movies, performances by great tragedians, mimes, and clowns and many more. This cornucopia of culture pouring into individual homes at the will of the home owner (and the price of a TV set) boggles the mind, especially when one remembers that only a short time ago, as history counts time, people were primarily dependent for news and discussion on newspapers, magazines, and pamphlets; for drama and music on theaters and concert halls; and for serious ideas and fiction on books.

With the explosion of mass media—particularly television—many people have argued that the importance of print and writing in our society has diminished. Marshall McLuhan once made the remark, "Print is dead," and many people, failing to understand what McLuhan meant,[1] took that statement literally, and have become advocates of "visual literacy," the media counterpart of reading and writing. "The generation of tomorrow will do its communicating with videotape, not pencils," some have claimed.

Certainly the future of electronic communications in this country is enormously exciting. In the past twenty-five years we have seen the use of one medium, the telephone, become a common substitute for letter writing, particularly over "long distance"; when you can "dial it yourself" and talk for three minutes for less than a dollar, why write? The use of computer terminals, home video, tape cassettes, videophone, and hundreds of other electronic devices will continue to expand dramatically during this century and the next. Clearly one needs to be not just visually literate in our society, but electronically literate; and we suspect that children in coming generations will be able to use computer terminals with as much ease as many of us use the typewriter.

However, print and the art of writing are hardly dead. One can cite statistics (the number of books being published in this country, the quantity of magazines published weekly) to suggest that the overall quantity of print in this country is increasing, not decreasing. In fact, the publishing industry has also benefited from the technological revolutions. Computerized photo-typesetting and offset printing aid in the speed and efficiency with which printed materials are produced, and in contrast to other media, print is cheap and becoming relatively cheaper. Further, as study of your own habits will probably reveal, most people are almost constant consumers of print. You may stay "glued to the tube" for hours on end, but you see print almost constantly from morning to night, including the time you are engaged with TV.

In many respects, the debate over various communications media and their importance is somewhat academic. One can argue on a whole series of questions—"Is the movie 'better' than the book?" "Are films 'better' than TV?" "Is videotape more 'real' than film?" "Is print dying?"—and still evade fundamental questions about language in school and society.

Print is here to stay; so is video and film and radio . . . not to mention conversation, debate, gossip, harangue, and invective.

---

[1] McLuhan was not declaring the death of the alphabet; he was simply suggesting that the "linear thinking" promoted by writing had been broken down by the kind of multiple, nonlinear thought made possible by electronic media. Margaret Mead's assertion about the changing thought patterns of the young (see Chapter 7, "Causes and Commitments" makes essentially the same point.

(So, too, it might be added, are thinking, imagining, loving, and fearing, along with the language human beings use to describe them.) The important thing, it seems to us, is not the comparative value of particular media, but the quality of literacy which underlies all communication.

For instance, in spite of the mind-boggling possibilities of an electronic marvel like TV, the fact is that the programs that pour forth from it stupefy and stultify the mind. In the race to capture mammoth audiences in order to sell a sponsor's frequently unneeded and unwanted products, the quality of programs is aimed at the lowest common denominator of interest and intelligence. Canned programs with canned laughter fill up the time slots. It is not uncommon for a prospective viewer to turn from channel to channel on his TV set and finally turn it off in disgust because the programs are vacuous, empty, advertisement-ridden, innocuous, and stupid. TV has been called a wasteland, and many potential viewers would agree. There seems to be a poverty of intelligence and courage—alongside a crass commercialism—that reflects an image of our culture both repellent and discouraging.

The greatest poverty of TV appears to be a poverty of the imagination. At one time in its history TV filled up its hours with quiz shows, without meaning or shape or creativity. Many of these continue. But even the dramatic shows are often devoid of imagination, with dialogue that has a phony ring and values heavily weighted toward the sentimental and romantic. Programs devoted to ideas or political debate too often turn out to be empty of ideas, remote from the real issues of the society, and are simply slick performances aimed at basic emotional appeals—to latent fears, hostilities, hatreds.

America as Seen through the Eye of the TV Tube

1. Most people who work for a living (and they are few) are executives and/or work in some kind of office.
2. Sex is the basis of all psychological, economic, political, historical, social—in fact, known problems of man.
3. Sex is very bad.
4. Sex is very good and the solution to all psychological, economic,

> political, historical, social—
> in fact, <u>known</u>—problems of man.
> 5. The present social order is here
>   forever and this is the best of
>   all possible worlds.
> 6. The present social order is here
>   forever and this is the worst of
>   all possible worlds.
> 7. The present social order is all in
>   the mind.
> 8. Women are idiots.
> 9. Negroes do not exist. . . .
> LORRAINE HANSBERRY, *To Be Young, Gifted and Black*

What has gone unnoticed, or at least unheeded, by the organization people of the electronic media, is that any medium, no matter how marvelous in extending human senses, is still dependent on human imagination, and that imagination is dependent primarily on language. As we have suggested in earlier chapters, we think literacy—print literacy, visual literacy, electronic literacy—springs from a fully developed and independent self, from a person who has a sense of the creation of self and who can interweave that self with the world at large, communicating freely and successfully with others, but doing so with imagination, freshness, and originality.

DISCUSSION

Do you agree with those who say television is a "wasteland"? If you do, what do you think this says about the values and morals of those who keep television afloat—the viewers?

Is print dying? How much time do you spend reading, versus being engaged with other media?

Are there any areas in your life where print is irreplaceable?

McLuhan said, "the medium is the message." What messages do the various media—film, TV, print, recordings, radio—transmit most successfully?

Explore the impact of the phonograph (and tape recorder) on modern music. How have the means (or media) shaped the substance—the music?

IDEAS AND EXPERIMENTS

Observe a daily news program on TV for a period of a week and write an account of the impact of the program and how it is achieved. Explore the editorial point of view manifested in the selections of news items, the method of reporting them, and the selection of pictures. It has been said that a picture is worth a thousand words. Is this saying borne out by TV news presentation?

Evaluate the quality of one of the talk shows; or evaluate the level of discussion of ideas on one of the interview shows in which a public figure responds to questions.

If you have an educational TV station in your community, watch it for a period of time and make a critique of its successes and failures.

All TV and radio stations are supposed to devote a number of hours of time each day to public-service broadcasting. Usually this broadcasting is put on when audiences are the smallest. Check up on your local station's public-service broadcasting, and write an account of what you discover. Is the station genuinely devoted to "public service"?

FURTHER POINTS OF DEPARTURE

Write an essay with your camera: Create a portrait of your family life, a study of your neighborhood, a profile of your town. Take a series of photographs that characterize in a coherent way some area of experience with which you are familiar. Arrange the pictures in an intelligible sequence, using a minimum of written language to lead the reader to the impression that you want to achieve. Then, write the same essay in words rather than pictures. Make a comparison of effects: Explore the differences, with particular attention to the possibilities in one medium not present in the other.

If you have a movie camera available, try shooting a film that makes some kind of statement about the world, about life, or about experience. A day in the life of a student. A day in the life of a mother at home, involved in the routine of housekeeping. Kids playing games in the neighborhood (fun, arguments, fatigue). Extremes of wealth and poverty in the city. Advertising as it mars and shapes the local scene. Think up

your own subject, and start shooting. You might want to work
up a narrative to accompany the film, or you might want to
use the reading of a poem or a recorded piece of music.

Select a poem that you like and attempt to capture its mood in a
sequence of slides or in a motion picture. You might begin
with a simple poem and capture its meaning visually in abstract forms; or you might begin with an abstract or highly
suggestive poem and give it meaning through concrete,
identifiable images.

Videotape equipment is now readily accessible to many people,
including the use of public-access channels of cable television.
If you can obtain the use of a small video outfit, explore the
medium by producing a show—drama or documentary, serious or satirical. Based on your experience, assess the potential
and limitations of the medium.

79 80 9 8 7 6 5 4 3 2